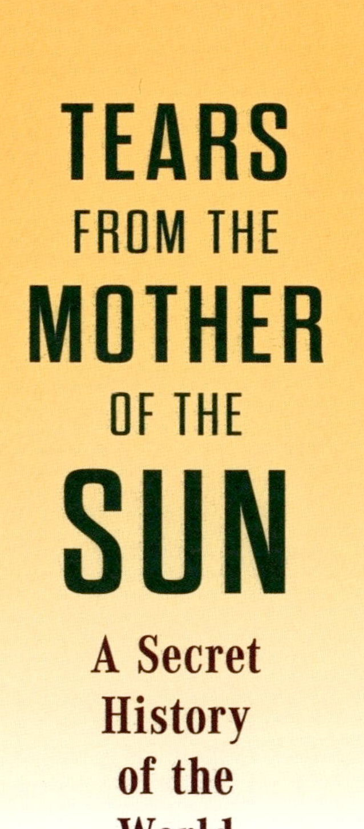

TEARS FROM THE MOTHER OF THE SUN

A Secret History of the World

A Sacred Planet Book

PIR ZIA INAYAT KHAN

ILLUSTRATED BY AMRUTA PATIL

Inner Traditions
Rochester, Vermont

Inner Traditions
One Park Street
Rochester, Vermont 05767
www.InnerTraditions.com

Sacred Planet Books are curated by Richard Grossinger, Inner Traditions editorial board member and cofounder and former publisher of North Atlantic Books. The Sacred Planet collection, published under the umbrella of the Inner Traditions family of imprints, includes works on the themes of consciousness, cosmology, alternative medicine, dreams, climate, permaculture, alchemy, shamanic studies, oracles, astrology, crystals, hyperobjects, locutions, and subtle bodies.

Cataloging-in-Publication Data for this title is available from the Library of Congress

ISBN 979-8-88850-182-5 (print)
ISBN 979-8-88850-183-2 (ebook)

Printed and bound in India by Replika Press Pvt. Ltd.

10 9 8 7 6 5 4 3 2 1

Text design and layout by Priscilla Harris Baker
This book was typeset in Garamond, with Dharma Gothic, Gill Sans, Gitar Latin, and Skolar Latin used as display typefaces

To send correspondence to the author of this book, mail a first-class letter to the author c/o Inner Traditions, One Park Street, Rochester, VT 05767, and we will forward the communication.

TEARS FROM THE MOTHER OF THE SUN

"Includes tears from Isis after Osiris's murder, tears of Adam and Eve, and tears of Avalokitesvara among the many vessels of wisdom in this book. It etches more than sixty episodes marking spiritual heroes and heroines across time and space, from Persia to India to Egypt, with a glossary to help navigate the lofty tales and apt poems that grace its pages."

BRUCE B. LAWRENCE, PROFESSOR EMERITUS OF ISLAMIC STUDIES AT DUKE UNIVERSITY

The bringing of light
is no simple matter.
The offering of flowers
is a work of generations.

Ursula K. Le Guin

Contents

The world before the subsidence of Atlantis and Mu.

Gentle Reader: The astral narrator of the greater part of this book sometimes has recourse to terminology proper to other ages, other lands, and other worlds. For your convenience, a glossary is provided at the back of the volume. Words defined in the glossary are marked with an asterisk when they first appear in the text.

Prologue

When the violet shroud of night fell over Tus, Firdausi again succumbed to bitter thoughts. A guttering lamp was the room's sole furniture. The poet's shadow shivered on the cracked plaster of the wall. Outside, a bulbul* moaned.

Memories welled up in waves. The early years given over to wine, women, and song . . . his truculent son, dearer now in death than he had ever been in life . . . the nights his pen had flown and the days it had stumbled . . . above all, the enduring tutelage of the daimon.

Where are you, Sorush?

A tuft of rue-smoke singed the air. Firdausi drew a sharp breath, squinted. The daimon appeared in a burst of flame. "At your service, Mir Abu'l-Qasim."

The poet paused to find words. "Sir, your kindness is the only balm I know in this world. But I fear my affliction is beyond cure. The Sultan has no time for our *Book of Kings*. The vipers of the court have poisoned his ear. There will be no dowry for Afsaneh. A little purse of dinars was thought sufficient to convey His Majesty's munificence. I gave the dismal sack to a bath attendant and quit Balkh before dawn. My hope has died."

The daimon's voice was an amiable rumble. "Then let it resurrect. Your daughter will prosper. In a month's time your body will be carried through the Razan gate to the graveyard just beyond the city walls. At the same moment, forty camels heaped with indigo will pass through the Rudbar gate seeking your door. Such are life's ironies. Art is honored in posterity. Why seek honor? Seek truth."

"Sir, I submit to your judgment in this and every matter. But isn't our epic a peerless piece of truth?"

"Rest assured, you have written an immortal book. But consider this. History consists of more than the deeds of kings. *Indeed, kings, when they enter a city, ruin it.* The real civilizers are the sages."

Firdausi reflected for a moment, then spoke. "My days of versifying are over and my life is near its end. For years you filled my mind with palaces and battlefields. If you find me worthy, unveil for me the caves and eyries of the adepts. Before I die, show me the true shahanshahs* of the world."

"So be it," answered Sorush. "Leave your pen aside and listen."

In the Name of God, the Most Merciful
and Compassionate

Egypt was in many ways the parent of Persia. For their sustenance, the people of that storied land have long depended on the fertility given to the soil by the yearly flooding of the Nile. In brief, the Nile guarantees the prosperity of the Egyptians.

But let me come to the point. There is a Nile of Niles that cannot be surveyed with eyes. When it overflows its banks, every field grows fecund. That hidden river is the Word pulsing through creation.

A river pours down from above,
Cascading from a dizzy height.
Its plashings sing of hallowed love
And never-ending life and light.

To speak of Egypt is to speak of Osiris. I will tell you in due course how he was betrayed by his brother. At present, suffice it to say that Osiris was murdered and Isis, his wife, wept copiously. Her tears streamed down from Sirius, the star of her soul. Sirius was known in those days as the Mother of the Sun. Falling to Earth, the tears of Isis caused the Nile to surge. In this way greenness came to Egypt.

These circumstances have an inner meaning. Heaven deplores the brutishness in the world. The pearlescent tears the angelic* legislators send down in the name of the Deity are sagely souls. It's the presence of the sages, century after century, that keeps the Earth verdant and fruitful.

The Deity

Once there was no day or night, no here or there. The One was, and nothing else. Or rather, everything was hidden in the One. And so the One was hidden.

A desire arose. It was the beginning of all desire. Doesn't beauty always wish to see itself in a mirror? The One wished to see Its own Face. That was the beginning of history.

Unless You choose to show Your Face,
Nothing can ever come to light.

The One wished to see Its own Face. That was the beginning of history.

Your Countenance, diffused through space,
Is all that ever reaches sight.

The One sighed. The sigh became a voice and the voice became a radiance.

You sigh, and from Your sigh flows soul;
You utter "Be," and there is breath.
Elixir pours into a bowl,
The goblet known as life and death.

In the Beginning

The sigh of the One is the soul of the universe and the mirror of the August Face. Soul became mind, mind became body, and so the world was made.

The One exhaled a sweeping sigh
Of such enormous amplitude
That from it came the starry sky
And all the planets' plenitude.

It must always be borne in mind that the cosmos is a person. Everything is a particle of that colossal personality. Its atoms are the stars. You and I are motes inside its motes.

This sky and light, these seas, this earth
Are breath and heat and blood and skin.
Behold the being of massive girth
Whose flesh and soul we live within.

The Hosts of Heaven

The angels were the first creatures. The foremost angels are called "the near ones."* They have never ventured far from the old fountainhead. It's difficult to distinguish them from the background against which they move; they hardly know themselves. They murmur "Holy, Holy, Holy," and then fall into a silence that lasts eons.

The later angels roamed farther. In those days there was space but no land, ocean, atmosphere, or stars. And so the angels flew in the emptiness of the void. They still fly there. When they meet, they glide through each other. The frisson of their touch is something exceedingly strange. Think of a hand lighter than air touching another.

Unlike yourselves we wear no mask,
Hence from us comes the perfect kiss.
If anyone should ever ask,
Then tell them that our touch is this.

◀ *When they meet, they glide through each other.*

Marij

After the angels came the jinns,* my people. If angels are light, jinns are fire. But our fire is not the fire you know; ours is cool and smokeless. We call it Marij.* It's the proverbial garden in the midst of flames.

The realm of the angels is called Jabarut.* Jinndom is called Malakut.* Malakut has as many climates as your material Earth. At its center, Mount Qaf rises up from the dense world below and ascends to Jabarut above, culminating in a resplendent peak known as the Emerald Rock.

Among the angels, strife is unknown. With jinndom it begins. We take the view that, for all their jarring dissonances, our elaborate polyphonies outshine the naive monophonies of the angels. Granted, the point is debatable. In any case, it's in our world that problems begin. And with them, novel prospects.

In Heaven's lanes pure peace prevails,
While lower down, discord appears,
Since wanderers on jinnic trails
Are prone to ardent hopes and fears.

Your Earth is an annex of the jinnic world, just as our

◀ *They took on ethereal bodies and reveled in the gusts and gales of the nascent planet.*

world is a purlieu of the angelic realm. For many of our folk, your territory repels more than it allures. The sheer weight of matter poses a predicament for us. Be that as it may, there are those who are fascinated by the grit of it all. Venturesome jinns migrated to the Earth before humans appeared. They took on diaphanes*—ethereal bodies—and reveled in the gusts and gales of the nascent planet. They are known as elementals.*

Among the rocks, gnomes play their games*
While undines swim in azure lakes,*
And salamanders crawl through flames*
As sylphs ride breezes through the brakes.*

Of Angels and Elementals

For a long time the Earth was only sea and storm. Then land reared up and verdure spread. The weather calmed and animals found homes in every nook and crevice of the globe. The elementals likewise swelled. As their numbers surged, alas, a faction became obstreperous and noxious. They bludgeoned their prophets, Amir and Saiq. A delegation of angels was dispatched to quell them, and was met with outrageous violence. Thus began the war of the angels and the elementals.

An angel finer than thin air
Is still a consequential foe;
Angelic light, a thing so fair,
Can fast become a blinding snow.

In the end, the wayward elementals were subdued and treaties were signed. The war was over. But let me not omit a significant detail. During the conflict, a precocious elemental boy lost his parents and came under the protection of the angels. Raised in the heavens, he came to be known as Iblis. So faithfully did he serve Heaven that he was awarded a diadem encrusted with a hundred-angled fragment of the Emerald Rock.

Through a Glass Darkly

There was peace again, but still the world was not free of confusion. The thoughts of jinns are "scintillas,"* a kind of psychic bacteria. The Face of the One constantly emanates flashes. Scintillas cluster around these rays, interpreting them in swirling patterns of phosphorescent dust. The resulting images outlast the bursts they answer. Often they are gleaming tributes. But sometimes they are grotesque distortions. A "figment"* is an effigy of the Deity that has taken on an ersatz life and motive force. Some who zealously quote God are in reality under the spell of a disingenuous simulacrum.

The thoughts of jinns are scintillas, a kind of psychic bacteria.

Such, alas, was the fate of the brilliant but troubled Iblis. He became a magnet for figments of dubious intent.

The One is not a thing of thought,
To know the One is not to know.
So put aside what you were taught
And separate the real and faux.

The Messenger

A council was convened to watch over the purity of the epiphanic rays. The Diwan,* it was called. An overwhelmingly luminous figure presided at the center of the convocation: the Messenger. Here was a personage who seemed to express in every gesture the radiance from which the tricosm* was made.

With light, however, comes shadow. Observing developments from a distance, Iblis found himself ineluctably drawn to the calling of Adversary.

Within this vale of mortal life
Nothing exists without a foil,
And so it is that love and strife
Compete as water does with oil.

As Azrael took our clay from the Earth, so he will return it one day. ▶

The Clayling

The Diwan discussed a newly arrived directive. A lush garden had sprung up in Jinnistan, an oasis of unrivaled elegance. It was to serve as the place of inception for a new kind of being. The archangels were instructed to bring a portion of clay from the Earth.

Alert to what was afoot, Iblis preceded them. He approached the Spirit of the Earth and planted in her mind a seed of fear.

When Gabriel arrived, Earth refused to cede him a piece of her substance. Michael, coming afterward, fared no better. Then Azrael came. He soothed Earth's trepidation and obtained the needed clay. Azrael's light touch won him the assignment, henceforth, of taker of souls. Just as Azrael took our clay from the Earth, so he will return it one day.

This clay we wear is not our own,
Its owner is the spinning globe.
Our flesh and bones are but a loan,
A transitory borrowed robe.

In the Garden, the clay brought by Azrael was molded into a form. The likes of that form had never been seen. Still, all who inspected it found it oddly familiar. The hallowed breath of the One poured into the lungs of the effigy and it arose with a start. Thus was born the Clayling, the first human being.

The Price of Pride

The angels were summoned to pay their respects. One by one they bowed on the ground in front of the marvel. When the turn of Iblis came, he remained stiffly erect. And so he gained the title "the Accursed."

Stay humble in the path of God
And love will ever guide your way.
To posture as a demigod
Is to announce you've gone astray.

When Iblis next appeared in the empyrean, Michael confronted him. A scuffle ensued, and Iblis's crown toppled from his head. The central emerald became dislodged, tumbled to Earth, and clove in two. Try as he might, Iblis was never able to find either of the shards.

Paradise

The Garden was a place of almost unimaginable loveliness. Four crystalline streams meandered between perpetually blossoming stands of frangipani, mimosa, and champak. Each morning, birds of incandescent plumage warbled exhilarating hymns to the dawn. When the sun reached its zenith, zephyrs wafted through the bowered groves, perfuming the air with heart-ravishing balsam. At night, shimmering rays streaming down from Sirius, Canopus, and Arcturus intermingled in traceries of breathtaking intricacy. If paradise was anywhere, it was here.

For all that, the Clayling was lonely.

A rosy plum is nectarous,
But sweeter is your dimpled face.
These flowering vines are decorous,
But I prefer your arms' embrace.

Seeing the need, the Deity split the Clayling in half. Where there had been one epicene individual, there now stood a contrastingly gendered pair. Adam and Eve, they were named. At the same moment, the Garden quietly transplanted itself from the soil of Jinnistan to the ether-sediment of the Earth.

◀ *Where there had been one individual now stood a contrastingly gendered pair.*

A Fateful Choice

Two strange trees grew in the Garden. The first, the Tree of Life, bore an ivory-colored fruit. The second, the Tree of Knowledge, produced a fruit red as blood. Eve and Adam were duly warned not to eat the vermilion fruit. Somehow, however, it was destined for them.

Iblis sent a serpent to tempt them. In truth, little persuasion was needed.

Had they eaten the fruit of the Tree of Life, they would have slept and awoken in the heaven of Illiyin.* As it was, with fingers and lips stained red, they opened their eyes in the mundane world, the valley of toil. The idyll of the Garden had run its course.

Your eye may wander to a fruit,
But pause before you take a bite.
Straight down from glory runs a chute;
Reflect upon the exile's plight.

To be sent out of the Garden was a shock and a blow. Earth's stark horizons and gaping chasms suggested intimations of menace. Huddled in a makeshift shanty, Adam and Eve brooded long over what had been given to them formerly, and what they had done.

◀ *Two strange trees grew in the Garden.*

A house of worship with the Black Stone as its hallowed centerpiece.

The tears the pair shed became puddles, then pools. Animals came to drink at these watering holes. Whenever they met the weeping couple, they offered their sympathy and encouragement. In deference to the animals' reassurance, Eve and Adam ceased their lamentations.

Day by day, a peculiar flame grew within their hearts. It was a flame of contrition, but also of enduring hope. Most of all, it was the shining sign of a devotion to the Deity that was now unquestionably earnest and sincere.

One day Gabriel and Michael arrived with the news that all was forgiven.

Do not forever live in shame;
Repair the breach, ablute, and pray.
Believe in the Forgiver's name;
Tomorrow is another day.

A great vision was then given to the pair. On a vast plain they saw an almost limitless assembly of people, displaying every imaginable cast of face, tone of skin, and length of limb. At the center of the throng was the indescribable presence of the Deity. A question now rang out: “Am I not your Liege?” Intense light suffused the atmosphere. Without exception, every voice in the multitude responded, “Yes.”

Angels inscribed the covenant on an olive leaf and sealed it inside a black meteor. To memorialize the momentous event, Eve and Adam built a house of worship with the Black Stone as its hallowed centerpiece.

Perfect Nature* Unveiled

Eve bore numerous children. Among them were Cain and Abel, who grew to become men of such fiercely opposed natures that their mutual annihilation was the result. Later years saw the birth of Norea and Seth, also called Agathodaimon. Favored by fortune, these siblings married in adulthood, and in time proved their parents' true heirs.

It happened once that Seth felt an urge to visit the now-empty Garden. Reaching the gate, he peered within. The sight that met his gaze was astonishing. The Tree of Life, with its white fruit, and the Tree of Knowledge, with its red fruit, had interwoven their branches. By means of this fascinating fusion a third tree had come into being, bearing fruit of an emerald hue.

If truth is what you would possess,
Do not divide reality.
Let life and knowledge coalesce,
Conjoining as a single tree.

A filmy apparition materialized beside the middle tree. Without a word the spirit plucked a fruit, extracted its seed, floated to Seth, and solemnly presented the seed to him as a gift. Seth received the offering with reverence. Taking his leave, he went and planted the seed in a fertile patch of ground. From it grew, in time, a marvelous tree laden with white, red, and green branches.

Enochiana

Among the descendants of Seth and Norea were three sagely siblings, a sister and two brothers. Their names were Sambethe, Asclepios, and Enoch. Together they formed a syzygy,* a molecule of prophecy. The children of Asclepios went west and gave rise, in time, to the civilization of Atlantis. Sambethe's children went east and seeded the flower that was Mu.* Enoch's children spread throughout the expanse between.

Enoch is also remembered by the names Fuxi, Enmeduranki,

Enoch taught his disciples the science of becoming animal.

Hushang, Idris, and Hermes. A beam from the palm of the archangel Metatron crowned his head.

Enoch taught his disciples the science of becoming animal. Under his instruction they learned to slip out of their bodies to prowl with wolves or wheel and swoop with eagles. This was possible because of the treaties Enoch secured with the Sovereigns of the Species. Enoch's people hunted animals, but only in a state of reverent ritual precision. The animals whose flesh they ate melded with their spirits under the aegis of the presiding Species-Sovereign.*

An animal, no less than you,
Possesses body, mind, and soul.
An ant, gazelle, or kinkajou
Is, like a human, fully whole.

On a fateful night, while Enoch was reciting the Name of the Deity, the heavens opened and he ascended through whirling mists, streaking comets, and blasts of lightning. He walked in halls of crystal and fire, conversed with jinns and angels, surveyed the Garden and its terrible antithesis. Flying around the moon and sun, he brushed shoulders with phoenixes and winged serpents. Gabriel then led him through a maze of constellations to the foot of the Exalted Throne.

When Enoch opened his eyes, words were ringing in his ears. A presence called to him, and he sought it in the wilderness. Suddenly it appeared: a ponderous slab of emerald protruding from the desert sand. Here was half of the jewel that had bedizened Iblis's crown. The dicta in Enoch's mind resounded more insistently now. He drew out his blade and began chiseling:

Truly, certainly, and without doubt,
The high is from the low, and the low is from the high,
Working the wonders of One, as all things were from One.
Its father is the Sun and its mother is the Moon.
The Earth carried it in her womb, and the Wind nourished it in her womb.
Fire will become Earth.
Feed the Earth from that which is subtle.
With great power it rises from Earth to Heaven
And becomes ruler over the high and the low.

Meteorites

The elementals observed the covenants being formed between humans and animals. They were of various minds. Some regarded humans as unwelcome interlopers and wanted nothing to do with them. Others were indifferent, and still others took an active interest in the newcomers.

Among those sympathetic to humans there were elementals who chastely guided and watched over them, and others who went so far as to pursue romantic liaisons with them. In the latter case, the motive was sometimes love, sometimes lust, and often a combination of the two.

These folk were here before we were,
And are our neighbors in this land.
Why should romances not occur?
Why should alliances be banned?

The result of intimacies between elementals and humans was the advent of a new, hybrid species. Flashing into sight one moment and invisible the next, these shimmering biracial beings brought to mind meteor showers falling from Orion. Hence they were called orionids.*

Like their elemental forebears, orionids lack physical bodies. In this way, they elude ogling eyes. Nonetheless, they carry a human inheritance and are for the most part well disposed toward your people. A good number of Earth's sages down the ages have been of the orionid race.

Still and all, romances between elementals and humans have not always proceeded on a benign track, especially in the early years. In the Enochian age, Harut, Marut, and certain other elemental thaumaturges* notoriously seduced human women with promises of initiation into sorcery, even while warning them under their breath of the consequences. Those who succumbed to the inducements of these philandering warlocks came under the sway of nefarious figments. In this way, baleful influences spread through the world.

Lapis Exilis

It was a time of chaos and confusion. The lineages of Enoch, Sambethe, and Asclepios stood strong, but mayhem was escalating. People began killing animals outside the bounds of sacred law. From unlawfully slaughtering animals to slaying fellow humans was only a small step.

Enoch sired Methuselah, and Methuselah sired Lamech. Lamech had two sons, Noah and Nir. More will be said of the illustrious Noah. As for Nir, he married Sothonim, who

Melchizedek unearthed an enormous emerald of the purest water.

afterward bore Melchizedek. Some say Melchizedek's father was not Nir, but a ray from the archangel Michael. Others maintain that Melchizedek was Michael himself.

When he came of age, Melchizedek went out to the wasteland. An uncanny patch of earth called to him, whispering cryptic bodings. A smaragdine fluorescence welled up from the sand and stones of the place. Melchizedek dug the ground and unearthed an enormous emerald of the purest water. This was the second shard of Iblis's crown jewel.

There lay the preternatural gem,
The flower of stone that long had graced
Old Lucifer's bright diadem
Till crown and jewel were both displaced.

Melchizedek went into seclusion. For long days he fasted and intoned orisons. Finally, clear instructions came. With tools of finely honed stone, he began chipping away at the shard. At last, the intended form revealed itself. The gem had become a seven-ringed, filigreed chalice.

With deference, Melchizedek presented the Grail to his uncle Lamech, who took great delight in it. When Lamech wished to see events on the other side of the world, he gazed into it and the desired scene was revealed. When Lamech died, his heir Noah presciently returned it to its carver's safekeeping.

Forgotten Lands

In the far west, Asclepios's descendant Uranus initiated a sacerdotal* dynasty. His uniquely capable daughter Basilea succeeded him on the throne and was hailed as the "Great Mother." Her fate, however, was not a happy one. A cabal of ambitious brothers assassinated her spouse and infant son. Driven to madness, she disappeared into a thunderstorm.

Basilea was succeeded by her brother Atlas and sister Hesperis. So monumental were Atlas's innovations that, in his honor, the realm came to be called Atlantis. Atlantis occupied a pair of vast islands in the Hesperidian Ocean.* Its influence reached from Mexico in the west to Egypt in the east, as the pyramids, mummies, and hieroglyphs of both lands attest.

The priests of Saïs kept its lore,
And thus was Solon made aware
Of the republic built of yore
Upon a fair Hesperid shore.

In the far east, another civilization was rising. Its builders were the descendants of Sambethe, sister of Enoch and Asclepios. The people of Mu erected cyclopean monoliths, formulated an ecstatic cosmology, and cheerfully roamed the archipelagos, islands, and atolls of the Ocean of Kiwa.* The sage Viracocha brought their culture to the Andes of southern Hesperidia,* founding the cities of Tiwanaku and Qosqo.

Volcanoes smolder high above
The teeming jungles midst the sea
That shelter the manuma dove,
And so endures Mu's legacy.

A Foiled Plot

Some say Norea, daughter of Eve and Adam, still lived in those days. Others have it that the Norea of later times was a descendant of the original Norea. In either case, the common name points to a common spirit.

Noah's tutelary angel Zophiel told him of the coming of storms of a kind so severe that the greater part of his native land would be quickly inundated. In earnest, he began to build a vessel of sufficient proportions to withstand the prophesied Deluge.

Beware a gloomy, leaden sky
Aswarm with clouds and streaking scud,
For it may be that, there on high
A tempest looms, portending flood.

Misguidance has a way of mimicking true revelation. To elicit a shipwreck, a wicked figment slandered Noah and urged those who came under his sway to build their own ark. The plans he provided were fatally flawed. Still, a group of naifs did exactly as the scoundrel told them, and a ship of sorts took shape.

Discovering the plot, Norea set the false ark ablaze. The figment appeared in all his grimness and attempted to subdue

and have his way with her. Breathing deeply, Norea called on the Deity. Forthwith, the angel Eleleth appeared in a flash of illumination, intoned Names of Majesty and Wrath, and drove away the villain.

Two great meteors hurtled from the Pleiades to the Earth. It was the beginning of the end of the beginning.

◀ *Discovering the plot, Norea set the false ark ablaze.*

The Deluge

The animals had revived the withered spirits of Adam and Eve. Enoch had won the confidence of the Sovereigns of the Species. It was unthinkable that Noah would abandon his feathered, scaled, and furred confederates to watery graves. He called the animals of the earth and air, and they came and boarded the ark.

Gabriel removed the Black Stone from Adam and Eve's temple and secured it in a vault in the mountain known as Buqbays.

Then the rains came. Earth became sea. For a year there was no sign of dry land. When a shoreline was at last found, it was found by a dove.

The raven first flew from the stern
And found no sign of verdant land,
But when the dove now took its turn
It reappeared with sprig in hand.

Much was destroyed in the Flood. Unicorns and gryphons were not seen again. Some say Atlantis and Mu were swallowed whole. Only those with swift and sturdy ships survived. Others hold that Atlantis and Mu were lost to other cataclysms. And God knows best.

A rainbow was the sign that life was to begin anew. Zophiel descended to teach Noah the hitherto unknown science of agriculture. Noah became a prosperous farmer and smiled contentedly over sprawling fields of tall, swaying corn.

Towers and Caverns

Beneath the three great pyramids of Egypt lie the tombs of Seth, Enoch, and Sab. Sab was a son of Enoch; from his line came the Sabians. In the days before the flood, Sabian adepts received instruction from seven hierophantic orionids: Uanna, Uanduga, Enmeduga, Enmegalama, Enmebuluga, Anenlilda, and Utuabzu.

The first of these, Uanna, was a merman. He emerged from the waters of the Persian Gulf each morning glistening with brine. His testament, *Enuma Elish*, narrates an arcane cosmogony.

In time the Seven Sages introduced Sabian anchorites to angels who taught them the lore of the planets and stars. As word spread of the influences of the spheres, towers were erected to better survey the heavens. The invention of cuneiform hastened the evolution of architecture in those days. With each passing decade, the towers grew higher and the astronomers peered further.

The true seers among the Sabians preferred mountains to towers. More often than not, they gazed at the firmament with closed eyes. In the hands of the uninitiated, however, the angels' starry wisdom degenerated into a crude astrolatry* devoid of gnosis. To raise their towers, the builders had recourse to forced labor. This was the beginning of slavery.

Finally, in a fit of frenzied ambition, the builders set to work on a tower intended to pierce the clouds and invade space itself. The Diwan disapproved in the name of the Deity, and the rising edifice tumbled to the ground in a cloud of dust that billowed for miles. From that day, the cuneiform of the builders came under suspicion. In its place new scripts proliferated, heralding new cultures.

A lord of slaves may build a tower
Or may erect a giant wall,
But lo! at last will come the hour
When all that Heaven scorns must fall.

In answer to the hubris of the tower builders, the mystagogue* Ishtar revealed another way. Her method was the technique of descent into the depths of the Earth. The initiates of her cult underwent an ordeal in subterranean darkness. Night after night, the mystai* purged themselves, until ultimately they were denuded of every trace of selfhood. They then returned up the steps they had descended.

Inanna's way is cold and stark
And teaches how to fade away,
For only those who know the dark
Can comprehend the light of day.

Gilgamesh, the herculean hero of Babylon, made the mistake of insulting Ishtar. Still worse, he and his orionid alter ego took the life of the presiding elemental of the cedar forest. These acts notwithstanding, the hermit Utnapishtim granted Gilgamesh an audience in the fastness of his misty island retreat.

Utnapishtim had lived for centuries, and had weathered the

Flood in a ship like that of Noah. When Gilgamesh pressed the recluse to divulge his secret, Utnapishtim explained that a seeker of immortality must stay awake in meditation for seven days and nights.

The hero, however, was not a gymnosophist;* he slumped over in sleep immediately. By way of consolation, Utnapishtim gifted him a rejuvenating herb. In his negligence, Gilgamesh lost it to a thieving snake on his way back to Babylon.

To strive for immortality
Is but to search for your own soul;
Beyond corporeality
Awaits the holy source and goal.

Kemet

Among the crocodiles, ibises, and nenuphars of the Nile, a profound civilization was upsurging.

The catacombs beneath the Great Pyramids housed the immemorial writings and relics of Enoch. The strangeness of the Sphinx signified the enigma of these antiquities; no one lacking the key would ever comprehend their mysteries. The guardians of the catacombs admitted their bewilderment.

Everything changed with the coming of orionids from the west. They called themselves the Kabiri, and spoke of a drowned continent. Carrying, as they did, the lineage of Asclepios, they were perfectly able to decipher Enoch's hieroglyphic instructions.

A book alone does not suffice;
The reader must be taught to read.
To cultivate a paradise,
First learn the way to rear a seed.

Enoch's path unfolded itself anew, and the pharaohs of Egypt walked in the antediluvian prophet's footsteps. Ptah and Sekhmet were first to rule, then Ra and Hathor, thirdly Shu and Tefnut. The successors of Shu and Tefnut were their grandchildren Osiris and Isis.

◀ *Isis wept voluminous tears and buried her bittersweet burden.*

Ptah and Sekhmet taught the use of fire. Ra and Hathor were personal disciples of Hurakhsh,* the angelic genius of the sun. To ensure equilibrium by way of contrast, Shu and Tefnut occupied themselves with the circulation of moist breezes.

The time now came for the art of sowing and reaping to be elaborated in full. This was the work of Isis and Osiris. The complexion of Osiris was green like the verdure that withers in autumn and regenerates in spring. Osiris's own death and resurrection conveyed the essence of his teaching.

The story goes like this. On a festive occasion, Osiris's brother Typhon brought out an oblong box and proposed a game. Each reveler was to take a turn lying inside. When Osiris's turn came, with manic speed Typhon slammed the door shut, nailed the box closed, dragged it away, and threw it into the sea.

Isis set out in search of her spouse. Friendly elementals pointed out Typhon's seaward route. At the shore, children indicated the direction the abductor's skiff had sailed. In memory of these children, to this day the Egyptians honor the wisdom that comes from the mouths of babes.

Isis eventually found the casket in Byblos, the capital of the Phoenicians. The box had washed up beside a tamarisk tree. The tree had grown to surround it, and had then been felled and raised again as a pillar in the city palace.

The colonnade in former years
Had been a seaside grove of trees,
And still to those with hearing ears
Its whispers were a bosky breeze.

To gain proximity to the pillar, in humble guise Isis offered her service to the queen, who followed the tradition of Ishtar and carried her name. Ishtar engaged Isis as the nursemaid of her infant son. The arrangement proceeded to the two queens' mutual satisfaction until, one day, Ishtar discovered Isis roasting the prince over a hot flame. Ishtar vehemently protested, compelling Isis to reveal her true identity and explain that she was merely coctioning the boy's aura with etheric fire, with no risk of harm to the lad.

But Ishtar had her own science of transmogrification, which she preferred. She therefore respectfully excused Isis from further service, offering her the guerdon of her choice. Isis, of course, requested the pillar.

Isis extracted Osiris's body, wrapped it in shrouds, and lachrymosely made her way with it down the coast. At Gaza she wept voluminous tears and buried her bittersweet burden beside the sea. A boy approached, furtively watching. As he came to her notice, Isis flung him a look of asperity, causing him to lurch and tumble into the surf.

Isis's anger departed as quickly as it had come. She helped the boy find his feet and laid her hands on his head. At that moment, a song burst into his thorax. He became the inventor of music; his name was Palestinos.

Beside the sea in Palestine
The noble art of song was born,
A soul-reviving anodyne
And sovereign balm for those who mourn.

But Typhon's mischief was not at its end. When Isis withdrew from Osiris's graveside, the brute exhumed the corpse and tore it into fourteen parts, hurling the pieces here and there as he ranged through Egypt. It fell to Isis to recover each fragment and give it a proper interment. In doing so, she established elegant shrines all across the land. In this way, the legacy of the siblings spread far and wide.

When birds consume the fruit of trees,
The seeds within fly far away;
And when a grain glides on a breeze,
A stalk will sprout downwind someday.

In the underworld Osiris became a masterful psychopomp, guiding souls toward their destinations with deft gestures of his crook and flail. On Earth, the hegemony of Kemet's pharaohs came to rest on the belief that as long as they lived they represented Horus, son Isis and Osiris. When they died and were entombed in glittering crypts they became avatars of Osiris himself.

The Oak of Mamre

Noah had three sons: Shem, Ham, and Japheth. Shem's progeny flourished in the oases scattered between the Nile and the Tigris, mingling freely with the Sabians. From the Shemites came Sarah and Abraham. Like Isis and Osiris, they were at once siblings and a couple bound in marriage.

Though originally of the city Ur, Abraham and Sarah lived for many years in Harran. In that hieratic city, Sabian priests had collected a set of twelve stones dispersed in the wreck of Adam and Eve's primordial shrine. For long generations they attempted to fuse these monoliths into a single Philosopher's Stone, alas without success.

The main preoccupation of Harran's priests, however, was the performance of solemn rites in seven monumental planetary temples of contrasting color and design. By means of theurgic liturgies, these astromancers routinely obtained the attention of the geniuses of the stars.

For their part, Abraham and Sarah gave their whole attention to Gabriel. When Gabriel appeared, he spoke only of the One.

A summons from the archangel uprooted Abraham and Sarah from the settled life they had so long known. As they rambled over hill and dale, a drought impelled their steps toward Egypt.

The adepts of the House of Atum were expecting them. In a

secret chamber, these mysterious hosts unveiled to their eyes the Emerald Tablet of Enoch and inducted them into the Osirian mysteries.

In Heliopolis of old
Sarah and Abraham were taught
To seal their eyes, and to behold
The Central Sun transcending thought.

When the procedures were completed, the couple departed the Nile valley. A third went with them: Hagar, a princess of Heliopolis, had entered into the communion of their syzygy.

In Palestine, people flocked to the hoary oak under which the entrancing figures of Abraham, Sarah, and Hagar sat in contemplative rapture. The three preceptors obligingly guided seekers in the way of gnosis, and the surrounding caves soon teemed with anchorites.

Some who sought instruction complained that their worldly duties made protracted vigils impractical. Following an impulse, Abraham walked to the sea and swam out to a rocky island. Amidst the shrieks of gulls, he declared the creation of an order of chivalry. The island was christened Sarras and a citadel was promptly erected there. Those who could not become troglodytes of the desert could swear an oath of valor and join the ranks of the knights and knightesses of Sarras.

The citadel of Sarras is
A fort of gallant fellowship
In which angelic promises
Are solemnized with blazing lip.

◀ *The hoary oak under which Abraham, Sarah, and Hagar sat in contemplative rapture.*

When Abraham visited Salem, the eminent Melchizedek heartily welcomed him. In a transport of elation the priest-king blessed the Urite prophet in the name of the Most High, served him a hunch of oven-hot bread, and made him drink from the cup he had fashioned from Iblis's crown jewel. Friendship was instantaneous, and Abraham and Melchizedek confabulated for days on end. In the end it was resolved that Melchizedek would take up residence in Sarras and there inaugurate a lineage of the Grail keepers.

Hagar bore a son; he was given the name Ismail. When the child reached his seventh year, the time came to divide the household. Trying as this parting was, it was necessary to prepare the way for coming generations. Gabriel's spoor led Hagar to the Arabian desert.

Setting up camp beside a bubbling spring, Abraham and Hagar discovered the traces of an archaic shrine. It was here that Adam and Eve had lifted up prayers to the Deity. The twelve pillars of the edifice were now in Ur, but a whisper in the air spoke of a still more vital stone. This was the voice of Sakina,* the spirit of wind whose presence is among the Deity's most dazzling signs. Sakina guided Abraham to Mount Buqbays, where he exhumed the Black Stone. And Adam and Eve's sanctuary rose anew.

Nomad that he was, Abraham came and went at intervals. Back in Hebron, it was now Sarah's turn to give birth to a son. The boy was named Isaac and, like Ismail, was destined to grow into a prophet. The progeny of Isaac would become the Jews, and the descendants of Ismail would become the Arabs.

The Jews and Arabs are both shoots
Of Abraham's great shady oak,
Which has its deep chthonic roots
Sunk in among an ancient folk.

Order and Chaos

The scions of Noah's second son, Ham, spread across Africa. In the west of the continent, the sages and heroes among these Hamites came to be known as orishas. They introduced arts and sciences, founded cities, and extended a protective wing over the people of their lands.

Female orishas as a rule spoke for the elementals of the waters. Oya, Oshun, and Yemoja had in their care the Niger, Oshun, and Ogun rivers. The sea and marshlands were under the aegis of Olokun. Among the male orishas were Obatala the city builder, Ogun the blacksmith, Orisha-Oko the farmer, and Olu-Igbo the forester.

The sciences we deem our own
Are no mere stuff of happenstance;
They have their roots in visions shown
In ecstasies of mystic trance.

The most influential of the orishas was Orunmila. A paragon of foresight and subtle discernment, Orunmila bequeathed to the Hamite nations the science of divination. All of the orishas attributed their skills to his instruction.

Orunmila's closest confidant was in almost every way his opposite; Eshu was a trickster of the most mercurial kind.

Orunmila had refined prediction to an art, but Eshu's presence always frustrated certainty.

The rule of law has its due weight,
But disarray must have its say.
It's true we're guided by our fate;
Still, chaos has a role to play.

One day Orunmila began to suspect that his companions were only interested in his bag of divinatory palm nuts. As a test, he staged his own funeral. Sure enough, one by one his associates came to his house inquiring about the bag.

Eshu was the last to arrive. When Orunmila's wife asked if he wanted the bag, Eshu shook his head; he had only come to commiserate. Orunmila at once leapt out and hailed Eshu as his one true friend.

◀ *Orunmila and Oshun.*

The Wooing of Shiva

The descendants of Japheth went east. Together with a contingent of Hamites, they crossed the sands of Arabia and Persia. At the foot of the Zagros mountains the tribes conferred. A spirited debate ensued and in the end the cousins parted ways.

The Hamites pressed onward to the east, in time reaching the pastures, paddies, and jungles of India, Serendib, and Kumari Kandam, where they contentedly settled. In these lush territories they domesticated buffaloes and elephants, grew rice, and zealously cultivated the arts of poetry, music, and dance.

Where tigers prowl and peacocks wail
There live a folk of umber hue
Who wear upon them, when they sail,
Long strings of pearls gleaming blue.

The Japhethites instead marched northward, pouring into the vast steppeland stretching from the Carpathians in the west to the Khingans in the east. Lake Baikal drew them with the twinkling of its wavelets and became their inviolable Sacred Sea.

But the Japhethites rarely stayed in place for long. Rovers by nature, they were given to a wanderlust that was not amenable to any form of restraint. Unsurprisingly, the Japhethites were the first

◀ *But how to court a yogi? The answer was yoga itself.*

people to compel horses to propel them on their way. Disdaining rooves, they slept in tents or under the stars. Camels carried their minimal effects.

This world is but a winding road;
Do not conceive yourself at home.
Let signs and wonders be your goad
And never cease to widely roam.

The steppe did not lend itself to agriculture, nor were the Japhethites inclined to dig the earth. While the Shemites and Hamites followed the example of the green-thumbed Noah, the descendants of Japheth resurrected the cult of Enoch and devoted themselves entirely to hunting in the day and shape-shifting at night. Their preceptors were shamans, accoutered with drum and rattle.

Among the Japhethites arose the legend of Shiva. The very sight of him was a phenomenon and a cause of alarm. A turban of dreadlocks crowned his head, a tiger skin clothed his ash-smeared frame, and a slithering cobra served as his necklace. In his right hand was a trident and in his left the skull-cup from which he drank.

Shiva was famed as both a hunter and a shaman. As a huntsman, he wielded a bow with such devastating effect that his name was never pronounced without the additional formula, "do not hurt me."

As a medicine man, Shiva was known as Lord of the Animals. The reason for this sobriquet was simple; Shiva was so closely allied with the patron spirit of animals that his word was taken as indistinguishable from the will of that great invisible authority.

In all the woods there is no beast
That lacks a spirit-paradigm.
Make Shiva, then, your trusted priest
And witness fur become sublime.

After years of wandering, Shiva took up residence in the Himalayas, in a spacious cave near the peak of Mount Meru. His sole occupation was the pursuit of an esoteric science of his own invention. By means of this technique, the feminine essence in the tailbone was made to rise and unite with the male essence in the pituitary gland. Posterity would give this procedure the name “yoga.”

Shiva’s only visitors were the fellow hermits who sought instruction at his hand. They pledged themselves ready to undergo the most harrowing rigors and self-negations if the prize were the ambrosia of enlightenment.

Seven disciples succeeded in mastering Shiva’s art: Atri, Bharadvaj, Gautam, Jamadagni, Kashyap, Vashisth, and Vishvamitra. These Seven Rishis personified the seven stars of the Great Bear.

The stars are not such far-off things;
They have their agents here below.
From Earth to Heaven run long strings
Through which celestial mandates flow.

The king of the mountains had a daughter named Parvati, “Mountain Daughter.” As soon as Shiva caught her eye she knew there could be no other husband for her. But how to court a yogi? The answer, of course, was yoga itself. For months she gave herself over to the most severe austerities. By means of Shiva’s method she generated so much heat that he could ignore her no more. The two were duly married, female and male principles reconciled.

Parvati was normally as mild-mannered as could be. When alerted to an abuse, however, her demeanor immediately changed. Her skin grew dark, her eyes reddened, and she shot out of her door with an implacable determination to throw the offender to the ground at the earliest chance. During these spells she was known as "the Black One."

Parvati is a gentle soul,
But do not earn her rightful wrath,
For perfect justice is her goal
And swift avengement is her path.

Just as Shiva had seven acolytes, Parvati had her own seven: Brahmani, Vaishnavi, Maheshvari, Indrani, Kaumari, Varahi, and Chamunda. They were called "the Mothers," and each embodied the essence of one of the seven Pleiades.

He of the Horns

When Shiva's peregrinations led him southward to the Himalayas, he took with him only a small band of companions, while the preponderance of his kinsmen continued to tend their flocks on the steppe. From this stock came the towering figure of Oghuz Khan.

From the beginning, the son of Kara Khan and Ay Khanum was a prodigy. Everyone remarked on his hairy blue skin, his massive proportions, and his resemblance to a bull. His parents struggled to supply milk and meat sufficient to satisfy his endless appetite.

Panegyrists contend that Oghuz Khan reached his full height in forty days. What is more sure is that, on reaching adulthood, he distinguished himself in striking fashion. An overgrown rhinoceros had been tormenting the tribe for years. Oghuz Khan seized the marauder by its spike and thoroughly convinced it never to show its face again. The next day Kara Khan bequeathed his mantle to his son.

Before taking his seat on the sheepskin of chieftaincy, Oghuz Khan went out into the wilderness, alone but for his horse and hawk. The sky was of a hue he had never before seen. A voice spoke, and he knew it for the voice of the Deity. "Command me, Tengri,"* he whispered.

"Call your people to Me," the voice answered.

Oghuz Khan closed his eyes and saw the brilliance of which the universe is made. When he opened his eyes, an enchanting maiden stood before him. He clasped her hand and she smiled.

There was something about his bride; she was a magnet. Oghuz Khan had previously commanded respect; now he attracted love. Soon he was the leader not only of his own tribe but of a confederacy of tribes. He told his vassals of the unity of the Deity and the virtues of meditation. The shamans of the land held a convocation and crowned him with a shaggy, two-horned helmet.

The horns that thrust out from his helm
Appeared as beams of lambent light,
For never in the steppish realm
Had eyes beheld a face so bright.

In Hyperborea, north of Baikal, the exposed flatlands of the steppe give way to a dense taiga of fir, spruce, and pine. The inhabitants of the forest were of a notoriously hostile disposition and caused constant vexation to the shepherds of the upper fringe of Oghuz Khan's horde. With a view to confronting these picaroons directly, Oghuz Khan ventured into the dappled paths of the northern woods.

A hush came over the foliage. Oghuz Khan closed his eyes; shapeless radiance filled his inner sight. A gentle song rippled from a nearby conifer. Oghuz Khan opened his eyes, approached the tree. Within a cleft stood a woman of surpassing loveliness. Oghuz Khan took her hand and she beamed. His syzygy was now complete.

◀ *Oghuz Khan and the sharers in his syzygy.*

When the people of the taiga learned that Oghuz Khan had won the hand of the dryad they so profoundly revered, they flocked to his side and petitioned to join his federation. He pressed them on the subject of their banditry. They stammered profuse apologies and confessed that their arctic neighbors, the Dog People, had influenced them adversely. They would now abandon all such miscreancy.

Oghuz Khan decided to call on the Dog People. These wolfish orionids lived in the gelid north of Hyperborea, on the far side of Mount Qaf, where in winter months the sun never rises.

On a lofty ridge, Oghuz Khan paid a visit to the fabled elemental griffin known as the Simurgh. Oghuz Khan listened with rapt attention as the Simurgh explained the geological processes by which Qaf's mineral arteries fed the many ranges of the world.

As Oghuz Khan and his retainers descended the northern slope of the mountain, the sky went dark. To walk sightlessly was a strange sensation, but the party proceeded onward undeterred. The darkness was not merely an absence of illumination; it was a palpable presence, an ink that stained all that it touched.

And in the center of the sky
An onyx sun sent down its rays,
The pupil of a jet-black eye
Effulgent with an ebon blaze.

The party made camp near a spring. Oghuz Khan throatsang by the fire while his cook, Yushi Hoja, went to fetch water. Yushi Hoja slipped on the bank of the source, drenched himself entirely, and climbed out sputtering. As he sat by the fire to dry, the party watched with startlement as his skin took on an eerie green incandescence. The glow was never to dim, nor would the cook ever die. He was known henceforth as Khizr, "the Green One."

The adventurers presently reached the land of the Dog Men. Predictably, the Dog Men greeted them with furious howls and a volley of arrows. Oghuz Khan stayed the hands of his men. Hovering behind the belligerents he made out the silhouette of a colossal figment of malevolent mien. Oghuz Khan gazed into the demon's eyes and pronounced the Name of the Deity.

At once the figment disappeared
And all the dogs laid down their arms,
For God Most High is deeply feared
By those who wield unholy charms.

The Dog Men proved amenable to reeducation. They had only served the figment because of the threats he had held over their heads. They were elated to be rid of his intimidation and regarded Oghuz Khan as their liberator. They embraced his creed with fervor.

In the years that followed, Oghuz Khan's confederacy grew by leaps and bounds. From the White Sea* to the Ocean of Kiwa, the prophet-khan's name was on everyone's tongue. What is more, his theology of oneness was on everyone's mind.

A final adventure remained. Word came from the east that a pair of elemental giants were wreaking havoc on the residents of an otherwise serene valley. Oghuz rode out to investigate. The elementals, Gog and Magog, received him with respect. They expressed their embarrassment at the reports he cited. Yes, perhaps they had done those things, they admitted. They lacked a coherent explanation but expressed contrition.

Oghuz Khan perceived that Gog and Magog would likely

misconduct themselves again. On the other hand, to punish them would be like condemning a stormcloud to a lashing. Gog and Magog were simply forces of nature.

An inspiration came to him. He conscripted every able-bodied person in the territory and directed them in the task of building a megalithic wall. Blocks the size of pachyderms were duly mined and fitted together so tightly that a mouse could not squeeze through.

When the partition was complete, Oghuz Khan called Gog and Magog and said, "This is the boundary you must not fail to respect." The giants nodded solemnly, and from that day onward all was well.

When Seraphiel's trumpet blows
Zu'l-Qarnayn's wall will turn to sand;*
Till then, as everybody knows,
It signifies the Khagan's hand.*

Dragonification

On the eastern side of Oghuz Khan's wall, but nonetheless beyond the reach of Gog and Magog, certain Japhethites abandoned nomadism in favor of a sedentary life along the verdant banks of the Heilongjian, Huanghe, Changjiang, and Zhujiang rivers. Just as Isis and Osiris had taught farming to the denizens of Kemet, the sage Shen Nong propagated five life-sustaining grains in the Land of Four Rivers. This land would come to be named after Chin, son of Japheth: China.

As ancient Eden had four streams,
So China has its rivers four,
Meandering through halcyon dreams
And irrigating epic lore.

As Oghuz Khan took his last breath, a child of monumental destiny was conceived in faraway Shandong. Queen Fubao was walking in the fields when a lightning bolt struck her, quickening her womb. The source of the bolt was no mere stormcloud; it was, in actuality, the star Dubhe in the constellation of the Great Bear. Twenty-five months later, on Longevity Hill, Fubao gave birth to a son. The child's face resembled that of a dragon, and he spoke immediately. Fubao named him Huang Di, the Yellow Emperor.

The moment that a child is born
The lines of fate shine from its face,
Foretelling how it will adorn
The world with its peculiar grace.

In his youth, Huang Di excelled in farming and the taming of wild animals. As time passed, it became clear that there was virtually nothing he couldn't do. He invented a script, minted money, mapped the stars, designed new fashions, and introduced the game of soccer. His knowledge of metallurgy and medicine was, in particular, profound and influential.

Huang Di was a disciple as well as a teacher. He owed his arcane knowledge to a pair of jinns: Xuan Nü, "Mysterious Lady," and Su Nü, "Clear Lady." Xuan Nü taught Huang Di military strategy, Su Nü taught him alchemy, and both taught him the esoteric techniques of amour, otherwise known as the arts of Yin and Yang.

There never rose a pedagogue
Bereft of any mentorship,
For wisdom's not a monologue,
But is, instead, a fellowship.

Huang Di's empress consort Lei Zu was also the disciple of a jinn. Her tutor was named Can Nü, "Lady Silkworm." From Can Nü, Lei Zu learned to manufacture silk. Lei Zu's lustrous brocades were the talk of the land; before long, faraway potentates were pining for silk wardrobes of their own. In this way the Silk Road had its beginning.

Shen Nong's descendant Yan Di, the Flame Emperor, reigned in the south. Having apprenticed themselves to igneous elementals, Shen Nong's successors had become adept in the use of fire for purposes both agricultural and military. Huang Di was troubled by Yan Di's repeated violation of his tribes' borders.

When all of his attempts at diplomacy were met with sneering rebuffs, Huang Di finally conceded the necessity of war. As expected, Yan Di's troops used torches and naphtha with harrowing proficiency. But Huang Di's aquatic elemental allies had prepared him well. He opened gigantic sluices and unleashed floods, so that the aggressors were washed away. Yan Di declared defeat and the two kingdoms were unified under Huang Di's benevolent scepter.

When fire is brought, do not bring fire,
But bring instead a cloud of rain.
Bring calm and be a pacifier,
And so assuage the burning plain.

Peace, however, proved long in coming. Jinns drew Huang Di into their feuds, Yan Di's partisans fomented revolts, and orionids marched on the capital. It was only thanks to Xuan Nü's masterful military counsel that Huang Di was able to stave off disaster.

When a lasting peace was finally realized, Huang Di knew it was time to lay aside his crown. He retired to the banks of the Jo River, where he immersed himself in austerities that gradually transformed his diaphane into the shape of a dragon.

Behind a person's outer face
There may reside another cast,
And out beyond the brink of space
This is the visage that will last.

Ex Oriente Lux

A band of roving Japhethites found themselves irresistibly lured eastward. It was as though the rising sun, glistening on the dew, had cast a spell over them. In an unbroken reverie of rapture, they glided through green thickets of boreal forest and slept under purple curtains of boreal light. A landbridge offered egress from the continent of their ancestors and all they had hitherto known. Onward they made their way.

The folk to whom the gleaming dawn
Extends its luminescent call
Are bound forever to be drawn
To eastern lands, as though in thrall.

Mountains and valleys undulated as far as the eye could see. Mammoths, bears, deer, sloths, lions, and dire wolves lumbered, slunk, and darted through the pines. As the migrants gazed at the teeming fauna of the woods and fields, the native elementals peered at them through the foliage with inscrutable glances.

In this boundless taiga the possibilities seemed endless. Some of the travelers built longhouses in the mountains and cheerfully renounced their wanderlust. Others, encouraged by the balmy promise of the southerly breeze, proceeded in the direction of Canopus.

◀ *Glooscap, Nukumi, and the Marten.*

There were still others, however, who could not shake off the allure of the Orient. They continued their eastward trek until they reached the Hesperidian Ocean's shingled shore. Here their epic voyage reached its terminus. They had found their solar Arcadia, their long-sought land of Red Earth.

So glowed the land incarnadine,
And so the beryl ocean shone,
That all was lacquered with a sheen
Which made a gem of every stone.

It was then that Glooscap appeared. In size and strength he was prodigious. Like the Yellow Emperor, he was born of a lightning bolt. He had a brother but, alas, that brother's ear was as attuned to the counsel of Iblis as his own was to the voice of Gabriel. There could be no meeting of minds.

A person may be your close kin,
Yet of a hard, deceitful heart;
Do not, then, join him in his sin,
But rather stay aloof, apart.

Once, while walking, Glooscap came across an old lady. She introduced herself as his grandmother Nukumi. By way of explaining her origins, she pronounced a riddle concerning the sun, a stone, and vaporous dew. Whether Nukumi was his literal or spiritual grandmother Glooscap could not be sure; he was in either case thrilled to discover her.

Glooscap noticed that Nukumi was malnourished and needed meat. A marten happened to be swimming nearby; Glooscap waved it over. "May I serve you to my grandmother?" he heard himself ask. He could hardly believe his own words, and was still more astonished when the marten assented without hesitation. As a crowning surprise, Nukumi instantly snapped the marten's neck and it fell limp.

A tightness gripped Glooscap's chest. His lips mouthed a prayer he had never before spoken, a supplication for the resurrection of the dead. Suddenly now there were two martens: the corpse on the ground, which Nukumi was already preparing to skin, and the marten itself, which smiled at Glooscap and declared itself the latter's friend for life. In that moment, a syzygy was born between the shaman, the fairy grandmother, and the animal familiar, never to be broken.

Search out a sophic elderess
And take up with a furry friend
To dulcify the wilderness
And help the world's ruptures mend.

Glooscap, Nukumi, and the marten went on to secure covenants with the deputy Species-Sovereigns of the land of Red Earth. A Golden Age henceforth commenced. His work complete, Glooscap paddled off in a birchbark canoe and was not seen again.

Snakes and Ladders

As I've said, only some of the discoverers of Hesperidia's northland went east. Many others advanced to the south. For long years they wended a course through bristling forests, chalky deserts, and prairies thundering with bison. Each hill and valley murmured its welcome. Those who yielded to the charm of a particular landscape solemnly took their leave of the others, and so the band gradually dispersed into scattered tribes.

The Bear Clan went wherever the blue corn led them, never feeling they had quite reached their destination. Their peregrinations brought them finally to the foot of a towering rose-red mesa. There awaited a figure wrapped in a rabbitskin robe, his head shorn and his face scarred with burns: Azrael.

It's true, his features are severe,
But do not rashly flee and hide,
For never will you find, my dear,
A kinder or a wiser guide.

The clan knew in their bones that they had reached the omphalos* of their dreams. They made bold to ask Azrael to be their chief. The archangel declined, but readily granted them the

◀ *Spider Lady was waiting. He recognized her for the venerable orionid wizardess that she was.*

land on which they stood. In the years that followed, kindred clans settled nearby, and in this fashion a nation was born.

Across the desert waste to the north, Mount Heart of the Earth overlooked the winding amble of Far Far Below River. Here the Puma Clan, distant kin of the Bear people, eked out their existence. Drought was a constant vexation.

The chief's elder son, Tiyo, was a peculiar boy. For hours he would brood in silence overlooking the Far Far Below. When he reached manhood he told his father that he wished to follow the river to its end. The chief knowingly nodded his head; it had been prophesied.

Tiyo floated down the river in a hollowed-out log. The current was placid on the whole, inducing a delicious languor. There were, however, moments when sudden accelerations sent the log crashing through fanged rocks or spinning through vertiginous vortices. In the end the river debouched into the sea and Tiyo debarked.

Spider Lady was waiting for him. At once he recognized her for the venerable orionid wizardess that she was, and performed an appropriate salutation. Summoned to her kiva, Tiyo set before her a bundle of prayer sticks, which she approvingly examined and accepted.

For four days Spider Lady plied Tiyo with dishes of cornmeal and filled his ears with auguries and admonitions. In the corner of the room, elixirs, philtres, and unguents simmered in pots suspended over a low flame.

Before a psychonaut descends
He must be properly equipped,
For no initiatrix sends
Resourceless hands into the crypt.

Finally the moment came. Accoutering Tiyo with a tuft of eagle plumage and a tub of ointment, Spider Lady lifted a mat to reveal a shadowed shaft furnished with a ladder. Tiyo descended to the subfloor.

The plumage sprang from Tiyo's hand and guided him through a plutonian maze of tunnels and chambers that seemed to never end. Scintillas whirled around him, some nightmarish, others exquisite. A viper of immense size nearly gored him until he pacified it by daubing Spider Lady's ointment on its tongue.

Tiyo found himself in a grotto beside the celadon Ocean of Kiwa. Tiny feet tickled his neck and he heard Spider Lady whisper, "There is the house of Sea Lady." A promontory rose up from the waves and Tiyo pursued it to the foot of a mansion of pink coral where a raddled crone awaited him.

The elderess received Tiyo cordially. It was not long before her spouse arrived: Hurakhsh himself. With Hurakhsh's appearance, Sea Lady was suddenly a comely young woman. Tiyo was now accorded an honor beyond all expectation; Hurakhsh flew him to the House of Dawn and instructed him in the mysteries of solar illumination.

Beyond the mountains to the east
There stands a great aubadic hall.
If you would serve there as a priest,
Then answer the aurora's call.

Spider Lady smiled when Tiyo returned and narrated his adventures. "One empowerment remains," she said, and set out with him to the east. As they walked, snakes proliferated. "Do not step on them," Spider Lady warned.

An old man greeted the pair at the edge of a village and

ushered them into his kiva. As a pipe of welcome circulated, the occupants of the room assumed the forms of snakes. Observing Tiyo's self-possession the elder commended him and offered his tutelage, to which Tiyo readily assented.

The elder was the chief and archpriest of his people. For four days he instructed Tiyo in ophidian mysteries of Atlantean vintage. A notable feature of these ceremonies was the persuasion they exerted on nimbus clouds, eliciting rain in otherwise parched times.

Tiyo's stay reached its culmination with his betrothal to the chief's daughter Tcuamana, a shamaness of high repute. When the nuptials were completed, Tiyo bid farewell to Spider Lady and the Snake folk, and led his bride to Mount Heart of the Earth.

The Puma Clan received the teachings of Tiyo and Tcuamana with reverence, and its corn fields flourished as never before. But with the passage of years a crisis befell. The people of the clan were aggrieved by the uncanny ways of Tiyo and Tcuamana's offspring, whose serpentine traits were sadly of an unexalted kind.

Tiyo and Tcuamana obligingly removed their children from the village and entrusted them to Tcuamana's relations. Having done this, they guided their disciples to the red mesa of Azrael. Perceiving Tiyo's mettle, the archangel welcomed the band. To this day their descendants perform their rites beneath the mesa.

Of Azrael much may be said;
His slightest deeds are notable.
He guides the living and the dead
With words forever quotable.

The Hero Twins

Japhethites were not the only settlers in Hesperidia. To the south, where the continent narrows and again widens, a flotilla slid into a lagoon fluttering with waterfowl.

The admiral of the fleet, Votan, was by pedigree a grandee of the Atlantean clan of the Serpent. A signal from the Diwan had dispatched him from his native island, Valum Votan, in the Antilles.

The company ascended the Usumacinta River, halting ultimately on the bank of a picturesque tributary. There they established the settlement of Snake Town. This little outpost would become in time the shining metropolis of Palenque.

Votan instructed his disciples to incubate veridical dreams in the jungle, with the aim of obtaining a nagual, or animal familiar. It might be a jaguar, a toucan, or perhaps an armadillo. Once the familiar was found, the alliance was lifelong. Some adepts forged as many as seven such bonds.

Now and then, Votan returned to his homeland. During one of these sojourns, he descended beneath the Earth and reached a subterranean sanctum pillared with helical stalagmites. There, in a flash of black light, he underwent a transfiguring catharsis.

In Valum Votan gapes a cave
That leads, at last, into a room

As silent as an antique grave
And redolent of rare perfume.

Back on the continent, Votan's final act was to erect a pyramidic temple beside the Huehuetan River. He built it, they say, by sheer force of breath.

Observe your breath and you will find
A current from another world
That surges through your inner mind,
Unfurling all that lies there furled.

Beneath the superstructure was a crypt called the Dark House, constructed in replica of the chamber of Votan's initiation. Here a portal opened between your world and ours.

For long years, the sibyls* of the temple conferred in the Dark House with jinns who were the spiritual elect of our people. With the passage of time, however, the successors of the earlier daimons slipped into ignorance and hauteur. They began to call themselves the Lords of Xibalba, and demanded plucked hearts by way of tribute.

A lineage that once was pure
Too often yields in time to rot.
The outer vessel may endure
But blighted corn now fills the pot.

Down the river, the brothers Hun Hunahpu and Vucub Hunahpu were always found on the ballcourt. Their grunts and shouts echoed miles away, causing the Lords of Xibalba no end of annoyance. One day, in a fit of pique, the Xibalbans lured the pair to the Dark House, tormented them with cruel pranks, and slew them.

As a concluding insult, the malefactors removed Hun Hunahpu's head and stuck it in the fork of a calabash tree. The tree suddenly burst forth in fruit. Unsettled, the lords issued a decree that the tree should be permanently avoided.

The maiden Blood Moon could not contain her curiosity. She approached the calabash and lifted her hand to Hun Hunahpu's leaf-encircled jawbone. Nine months later she gave birth to twins, Hunahpu and Xbalanque.

Growing to manhood, the twins were inducted into the mysteries of Votan and presented to the elders of the jungle. A venerable rat they met in this way led them to their father's old ballcourt. As soon as they began to play ball, the Lords of Xibalba requested the pleasure of their company.

Their father and uncle had made the mistake of visiting Xibalba unaccompanied. Hunahpu and Xbalanque wisely surrounded themselves with a band of feral allies. As the party made its way into the underworld, a mosquito, a macaw, a colony of ants, a coati, a possum, and a rabbit each lent a hand at decisive moments, so that peril was continuously repulsed.

It is our dedicated friends, indeed,
Who make the path of life worthwhile.
All others flee in times of need,
But these remain, mile after mile.

When a final showdown brought Hunahpu and Xbalanque face to face with their persecutors, the twins had recourse to Votan's profoundest teaching. They died and, like a pair of phoenixes, rose again.

The greatest trick that may be wrought
Consists of vanishing from sight

And, having dwindled down to naught,
Rising anew, suffused with light.

Thoroughly chastened, the Xibalbans swore to refrain henceforth from tyrannizing the land. It remained for the twins to honor their father with a suitable burial. Having fulfilled this filial duty, Hunahpu and Xbalanque ascended in spirit to the sun and moon, respectively.

The Gallows Tree

The founder of Palenque was the second of three Votans. The first of these was an archimage* who flourished in the golden age of Atlantis. In the course of that civilization's tumultuous decline, the school of this original Votan split into two branches. The northern branch took root in Thule, while the southern branch established its headquarters in the Antilles. We've spoken of the deeds of the southern lineage, but what of the northerners?

The third Votan was a hybrid, an orionid, as were his family and disciples. Let's call him Odin, the name by which he is better known. He was of considerable stature, wore a long beard, carried a pair of ravens on his shoulders, and had only one eye. Why only one eye? The story bears telling.

Rumor reached Thule of a land at the northern extreme of Rum,* where ice and fire were savagely contending for paramountcy. Frost had hitherto held sway, but blasts of thermal wind had lately liquidated previously impassable ice walls. Reindeer now freely roamed where before nothing had moved or breathed, and a gargantuan ash tree stood revealed at the center of the thaw. The Neanderthals called it Yggdrasil.

Fascinated by the reports, Odin consulted the Diwan and received encouragement to investigate the wonder; destiny

awaited him there, confirmed Gabriel. He set out at once, alone.

They said, there stands a peerless tree
Where ice and fire contend in strife.
Now this was something he must see,
And so he packed his cloak and knife.

The journey was perilous; sabretooths and thunderbirds were a frequent menace, and the defiles requiring traversal were rimed with treacherous hoarfrost. All of this notwithstanding, the wayfarer eventually reached his destination. The sight that lay before him repaid the hardship of the intervening miles a hundredfold.

Yggdrasil was enormous. At its crown, soaring foliage disappeared into the azure of the sky. Atop this pinnacle a splendid eagle made its nest. Below, the tree's spraddled roots sank deep into the recesses of the Earth. Here a primeval serpent lay coiled. Between the bird and the snake, an impish squirrel skittered back and forth, pretending to facilitate dialogue but in reality fomenting distrust.

A conversation tête-à-tête
By far outshines remote conferral.
A middleman is handy, yet
You're at the mercy of the squirrel.

Three springs irrigated Yggdrasil. The first was a favorite haunt of the serpent. Odin chanted a hymn here and moved on.

At the edge of the second spring, three elemental maidens held court. These were the Norns, sisters of profound perspicacity.

◀ *There stands a peerless tree, where ice and fire contend in strife.*

Their primary occupation was watching over the tree and regularly coating its roots with mud. Otherwise, they beguiled their time by weaving tapestries emblazoned with scenes from the past, present, and future. Odin paid his respects and walked onward.

Old Verdandi, with Urd and Skuld,
As Odin came and bowed and left,
In silence wove her cloth and mulled
The pattern of life's warp and weft.

Mimir, an enigmatic elemental, held vigil at the third spring. He was dipping his drinking horn into the water as Odin approached. Odin begged for a sip, but Mimir refused. Undeterred, Odin urged the jinn to name his fee. "The price is your eye," answered Mimir. Without flinching, Odin took out his blade, extracted one of his organs of sight, and dropped it in the spring. Mimir passed the horn.

If you would gain your true desires
Then do not shrink from sacrifice,
For reciprocity requires,
For every jewel, an honest price.

As Odin drank, the roaring pain in the ruin of his face abruptly ceased. He found that he could see through both eyes, the eye in his head and the detached one floating in the pool. The former showed him the familiar contours of the world. The latter revealed a world his hermetic visions had until now only faintly foreshadowed: *light upon light* in infinite regress, whelming the senses, engulfing the stars.

Mimir gave Odin a rope. Odin knew what to do. He climbed Yggdrasil, tied his feet to a lofty branch, and hung his torso down. For forty days, inverted on the tree, he intoned the Name of the Deity.

The serpent began slowly winding up Yggdrasil's bole. The squirrel fled in panic. The Norns smiled knowingly as rays flashed out from the eagle's nest. At last, the two powers were in direct contact.

The Grail in Persia

Let's return to the lands of the Silk Road. No one knows the story of the Iranian nation as well as you, Mir Abu'l-Qasim. You've chronicled it in superb detail in your *Book of Kings*. But I would like to amend the information I previously supplied. That was the official version; this is the secret history.

Your epic names Jamshid as the son and successor of the majestic Tahmuras. That is, of course, the standard account. But what if I were to tell you that Jamshid was actually born in a backwoods hut?

Perhaps you've heard the tale before
A dozen or a hundred times,
But have you heard the untold lore,
The hidden twin with which it rhymes?

Yes, Jamshid was a Japhethite nomad. How, you will ask, was he hoisted to kingship?

One day as he tended his flock, a raven alighted on a nearby outcrop and urged him to go and preach the law of Heaven. Jamshid demurred, insisting that he was not cut out for evangelizing. Jumping from one foot to the other, the raven suggested that, in that case, he ought to make the land prosper. To this proposition Jamshid agreed.

◀ *Jamshid peered into the depths of the goblet and saw a scene.*

Do not assume a feathered beast
Is uninformed of wisdom's ways.
The karshipt raven was a priest*
Of glowing heart and piercing gaze.

For long years Jamshid labored to expand the fortunes of the clans in his midst. The earth responded favorably to his coaxings, and a verdant carpet unrolled across the steppe, festooned with scarlet poppies, coral tulips, and cerulean crocuses.

But, for every flow there is an ebb.

One day, Melchizedek's heir arrived from faraway Sarras. The Grail, he announced, was at Jamshid's disposal. Without a moment's delay, Jamshid peered into the depths of the goblet. In the plasma swirling there he glimpsed a scene of bitter cold, lashing winds, and stinging hail.

Stirred to action, Jamshid rounded up all who would listen and set them to work excavating an underground refuge.

The heart that knows of what it speaks
Speaks volumes in a single word.
An instant does the work of weeks
And hearers trust in what they've heard.

In this way a palatial cavern took shape. It boasted well-appointed suites, teeming corrals, twittering aviaries, and fertile fields overlit by a simulacrum of the sun. At night, a second orb replicated the moon. As soon as the haven was complete, the expected whiteout blotted out the world. For long years, Jamshid and his people kept to the shelter of their subterranean paradise.

When the door finally creaked open, earth and sky were as fresh as the first day of creation. An aura resembling a raven's glittering pinions flashed around Jamshid's head and shoulders.

No one could deny the sovereignty he held in trust from the Diwan. A belle epoque was now to begin.

The world had never before seen such a prolific patron of the arts and sciences. At Jamshid's instance, industrious crews dug quarries, planted vineyards, launched galleys, and erected pillars and domes of such colossal proportions that Ctesiphon, Jamshid's capital, soon attracted sightseers from the four corners of the globe.

Not even the notorious scofflaw Iblis was allowed to remain idle; Jamshid corveed him as his personal tutor in grammar. Truth be told, Jamshid was most at ease among elementals. His queen consort and sister's husband were both beings of this kind. The children of the royal house were all orionids.

In former times, that was the way;
Our peoples lived in good accord.
*Between the human and the fae**
A shared existence was explored.

The Grail continued to fascinate Jamshid. Probing its recesses, he traced a route between the planets, and a plan formed in his mind. On the morning of the spring equinox, he seated his diaphane on a pranic* throne and ordered his jinnic retainers to propel it into space.

On reaching the solar sphere, Jamshid held colloquy with Hurakhsh. This would be the first of several such interviews. Among the citizenry of Ctesiphon, the spectacle of the king's astonishing ascent gave rise to the annual feast of Nawruz.

It was then that Jamshid took a false step. On a fateful night, dizzy with wine, he recounted his many feats to peals of applause from fawning courtiers. At the climax of his auto-panegyric, he permitted himself to say, "No one in this world is my equal." Suddenly the hall fell silent. The assembly watched in horror as Jamshid's famed aura extracted itself, flapped its wings, and fluttered away.

Mistakes are rarely serious,
For all of us, we know, are flawed,
But what is deleterious
Is to compare oneself with God.

In the astral world, the councilors in the Diwan lowered their heads. The next morning, the news was brought to Jamshid that the Warden of Sarras had departed in the night with the Grail.

Revolution

Some regard the snake as an evil creature. But really, is any of the Deity's creations evil in itself? Villainy is a choice some jinns and humans make.

I have told you of Votan II, whose antecedents belonged to an Atlantean clan loyal to the Species-Sovereign of serpents. With the plunging of the continent, its folk were scattered to the four directions. A descendant of a line that went west came to prominence among the sorcerers of Babylon. This was Zahhak.

Votan II and the priestesses of Palenque cultivated auric serpents conducive to enlightenment. Zahhak was of another bent. The twin snakes that coiled around his spine and overtopped his shoulders fed on the fumes of his rancid caprices.

Two serpents climb the spinal cord,
Of solar and of lunar light.
Do not estrange them from the Lord;
Be sure their scales shine pure and bright.

Mir Abu'l-Qasim, your epic well relates the tale of Zahhak's rise and fall: how he usurped Jamshid's tottering throne; how he reigned from Jerusalem for many long, dark years; how the righteous blacksmith Kaveh sparked an insurrection; how the dauntless Faridun deposed the tyrant and immured him in the bowels of Mount Damavand.

The villain who cannot be changed
Must still be stopped from doing worse.
A mind that, sadly, is deranged
Should not be free to spread its curse.

Splendid as your telling is, it omits the part played by two notable protagonists. In the celestial Diwan, Anahita and Vayu represent the constituencies of water and air. One night, in a fit of malice, Zahhak drew sigils designed to bind these Heavenly ministers to his service. His aim was a flood to rival the famous Deluge. With rebuke in their eyes, the angel pair wriggled free of their bonds and darted away.

Faridun later propitiated the pair in the name of the Deity and they came to him at best speed. Zahhak had by then fled to India. Anahita and Vayu blasted Zahhak's guardsmen with a gale, so that Faridun made quick work of the remnant and seized the despot handily.

All those who, in their need, turn to
The Deity who made us all
Will meet with help from sweet Vayu,
And bright Nahid will hear their call.

Faridun had in common with Zahhak a knack for the magical arts. Unlike his predecessor, Faridun used his philters and incantations for purely generous purposes. Mounting the throne he became not only king; additionally and more importantly, he served as physician-in-chief.

The rule of Faridun was such
That one and all knew peace and joy.
To every soul, the monarch's touch
Brought happiness without alloy.

Iran and Turan

Faridun espoused his three sons to princesses of Yemen and entrusted to each a third of his empire. Salm was to rule the Greeks and Slavs, Tur the Turks and Chinese, and Iraj the Iranians. But Salm and Tur were dissatisfied with their lot. They slew Iraj and sent his head to their father as a token of their discontent.

However well a child is bred,
There never is a guarantee.
Alas, at times it must be said:
The apple's rolled far from the tree.

The heartsick king's only consolation was in learning that Iraj's widow was heavy with child. In due course she bore a daughter, and the daughter in time became a mother herself. Iraj's grandson, Manuchihr, was destined to defeat his wicked granduncles and restore order to the realm.

But idylls are fleeting. Manuchihr's son Nawzar lacked his father's qualities, and under his rule the kingdom soon fell into disarray. Only the valor of the paladin Sam staved off utter ruination.

Sam always conducted himself irreproachably, except in a single instance. When his son Zal was born with albinism,

he took the child's snowy complexion as a malefic omen and exposed the boy on Mount Alburz.

A sign from the Deity put the Diwan on the case; the Simurgh was charged with raising the little outcast alongside her brood of chicks. Like Isis, Simurgh had her numinous roots in Sirius. No one could have given Zal a more philosophically rigorous education.

Years later, Sam repented and reclaimed his son. Simurgh bid the boy farewell with the gift of three magical feathers.

Can any moment smite the chest
More fiercely than a last goodbye?
When new-fledged birdlings fly the nest
The mother bird can only cry.

Much of this tale is told in your *Book of Kings*. You tell there, too, with an expert touch, how Rustam was born to Zal and Rudabeh, and how he rose to immortal fame as champion of the realm in the time of Nawzar's heirs, the Kayanians. Had it not been for the peerless Rustam, Iran would have been engulfed time and again by its northern rival, Turan.

Kay Qubad, the first of the Kayanians, was formidable. As for his successor, Kay Kavus, you put it well in your immortal pages when you say that the leaves of his tree were yellow. You go on to describe how he attempted to pierce the veil of Heaven on a throne propelled by a quartet of eagles, only to hurtle to the ground. That is the story told in tea houses.

Now listen, this is how it really happened. Kay Kavus was the disciple of his younger brother, Kay Nishin, an adept of high degree. Under Kay Nishin's guidance, Kay Kavus undertook a

◀ *Simurgh was charged with raising the little outcast, Zal.*

solitary retreat. In his meditations, his eidolon* traversed the spheres. His concentration faltered, however, and he fell back into his senses, never to reach the same heights again.

If you would fly up through the sky,
Then listen well to this advice:
Retain an ever-steady eye
Or down you'll plummet in a trice.

Kay Kavus's worst instincts prevailed in his dealings with his gentle son, Siyavash. You know how it went. First there was the preposterous trial by fire, which Siyavash bore with admirable patience. Then the insistence that Siyavash indulge in unchivalrous perfidy, which no prince worth his salt could be expected to bear.

What could Siyavash do but accept the hospitality of his father's archfoe, Afrasyab, in the White Forest? Siyavash was duly joined in wedlock with Afrasyab's daughter Firangis, an alliance that might have reconciled the warring nations had Kay Kavus and Afrasyab shown themselves less bullheaded.

For a time, Siyavash lived happily in the land of the Turks. Afrasyab appointed him governor of Khotan, and he poured his energies into the construction of a castle with walls of gold, silver, steel, bronze, iron, crystal, and various precious stones. He christened it "Kangdiz"; some call it Shambhala. The magi* say that at the end of history, Zarathustra's heir will ride out from its gates.

The castle of the noble prince
Was built to serve divinity.
Its halls have echoed, ever since,
With whispers of infinity.

But Afrasyab's friendship was fickle. When jealous courtiers slandered Siyavash, he impulsively condemned his son-in-law to death. The prince was decapitated, and vermillion flowers sprang up from the soil tinctured by his blood.

The blood of martyrs is a juice
That nurtures gardens red as flame.
The wounds of saints always effuse
A fire that puts the sun to shame.

Siyavash's seed was in Firangis's womb. When the child was born, she named him Kay Khusraw and placated her father by sending the boy to be raised as a rustic in the mountains. Afrasyab would later rue his acquiescence to the plan.

When Kay Khusraw came of age, the Warden of Sarras brought the Grail and placed it at his disposal, opening his eyes to many things. Henceforth, Kay Khusraw spent his days marshaling knights and his nights deciphering the starry glyphs that shimmered in the cup.

An auspicious alignment of planets sent Kay Khusraw into action. Riding against Afrasyab under a thundering sky, he pursued him to Lake Chechast in Azerbaijan. Beside the lake he vanquished the killer of his father and erected a pneumatic fire by way of memorial. With great rejoicing, Kay Kavus anointed Kay Khusraw his heir. The aged king died soon after.

Worldly power held no charm for the shepherd-turned-monarch. As soon as the kingdom stabilized, he conferred his crown on a nephew. With tender words he bid farewell to the four sibyls who were the sharers in his syzygy.

Abandoning forever the luxury of Kangdiz, Kay Khusraw followed a trail leading into the mountains. His loyal paladins accompanied him, all the while urging him to turn back. At dawn he bathed in a crystal spring, intoning sacred strophes. He then blessed his companions and disappeared into a snowstorm.

And thus a dynasty was sealed,
A string of kings, now weak, now strong.
By Khusraw's hand the line was healed,
And glory was its final song.

Daughter of Earth

The Hamites of India nearly knew total obliteration. One fateful season, a merciless monsoon laid waste to their cities, leaving only the couple Manu and Shraddha to pick up the pieces. Ten of their children quarreled and destroyed each other. Ten others survived to repopulate the land. Of the survivors, two became founders of dynasties, one Solar and the other Lunar.

How many savage storms must rend
The fabric of this realm of ours?
Yet never does the saga end,
For dawns are numerous as stars.

For centuries, the Solar Dynasty ruled the kingdom of Kosala from a marmoreal palace in the city of Ayodhya. Dasharath, a scion of this line, ascended the throne when his time came. To his first wife, Kausalya, was born the incomparable Rama. The prince's education was supplied by the priest Vashisht, who bore the auspicious name and lineage of Shiva's sixth disciple.

When Rama reached adulthood, he found himself one day among a throng of distinguished suitors for the hand of Sita, princess of Videha. Raised by Maharaja Janak, Sita was not in fact his daughter. Her forebears were a breed of noble

hierophants who conducted their liturgies amidst congregations of ophidian orionids in amethystine caverns deep beneath Janak's acres. It was therefore said that Sita's mother was the Earth. When Sita's eyes met Rama's, she draped around his neck the marigold and jasmine garland that signified her assent. The two were married soon after.

Two hearts that share a tacit bond
Accede at once to blissful fate,
For as their feelings correspond,
Both recognize their destined mate.

The newlyweds were happy for a time in Ayodhya. Then, out of the blue, a bolt struck. One of Dasharath's wives extracted from him a wretched edict: Rama was to be banished to the forest for fourteen years. Without a word of protest, the prince departed. Sita joined him, together with his stalwart brother Lakshman.

The three exiles discovered that creek water was sweeter than sherbet and the squawks of parakeets more melodious than trumpets. Fourteen joyous years passed in this way. And then another bolt struck.

There always is an ending to
Our sweetest interludes of peace.
But be consoled, it's also true
That every woe will likewise cease.

In a quiet glade, Sita was startled by the greeting of a mendicant. Hardly had she answered when he revealed himself as Ravana, the elemental maharaja of Serendib. Seizing her in his

◀ *It was said that Sita's mother was the Earth.*

massive hands, he spirited her away to his hulking fortress.

Rama and Lakshman's quest for Sita was fraught with adventures. More than anything else, what speeded their success was the friendship of orionids resembling monkeys and bears. Among these furred and clawed allies, the ethereal ape Hanuman distinguished himself as Rama's staunchest champion. Ravana was at last defeated, and Sita rescued.

Rama duly mounted the throne of Ayodhya, and here the tale should have ended. But a third bolt descended, the worst blow of all. In the streets of the city, people of low mind bruited vulgar rumors concerning Sita's days under Ravana's roof. As a duteous statesman, Rama saw no option but to send her away. And so, once again, Sita went into exile.

Sita carried Rama's twins in her womb. She was fortunate to find haven in a hermit's monastery. When the boys grew to manhood, Rama appeared. He ardently wished to reunite their lives. As a means to this end, he proposed a test of Sita's faithfulness.

Sita consented, but insisted on administering the test herself. She announced, "If I was true, may the ground open for me." The earth ruptured, a stairway appeared, and Sita descended into the subterrestrial halls of her ancestors, never to appear again.

A princess born to earthly depths
Will not forever linger here;
At last she must retrace her steps
And, in her Mother, disappear.

With a deep sigh, Rama led his sons back to Ayodhya. Beside his throne he erected a second throne, and there installed a golden effigy of Sita. She would always be his queen.

Dark Allure

The afterglow of Rama and Sita's appearance ensured centuries of harmony and good fortune for the people, jinns, hybrids, and animals of Hindustan. But vice cannot be thwarted forever; pernicious figments will always have their seasons of resurgence.

In Mathura, the peace of the kingdom was shattered by Kans, a prince consumed with ambition. In a transport of brutish impatience, Kans threw his father in prison and insisted on his own coronation.

When Kans's sister Devaki married a nobleman of the Yadav clan, the proto-tyrant heard an eerie voice whisper that Devaki's son would prove his undoing. Accordingly, whenever Devaki bore a male child, Kans smothered it. Six innocent infants died in this way. The seventh and eighth survived only because Devaki secretly dispatched them to be raised by cowherds in a remote village.

When holy order wastes away
And darkness rolls across the land,
It's then that Heaven sends a ray
And godly guidance takes its stand.

The village priest gave Devaki's boys the names Balaram and Krishna: "Rama the Strong" and "the Dark One." The brothers proved astonishingly precocious. They quickly earned the status of village heroes by driving off malicious jinns. Krishna's prowess was tinctured with a vein of puckish mischief, but his playfulness only further endeared him to the villagers.

In the flower of his youth, Krishna's charm exceeded all bounds. When he played his bamboo flute, the cowgirls of the pastures abandoned their pails and flew to him. As thunderclouds roiled the sky and peacocks shrieked in the banyan trees, the milkmaids found themselves spinning around Krishna's dark form. The bells of their anklets rang out rhythms older than the hills.

When Krishna's flute emits its skirl,
The gopis run to join the dance.*
They laugh and sing and softly whirl,
Ensorceled in a mystic trance.

But do not suppose that Krishna was a wanton and a sybarite. On the contrary, he was perpetually absorbed in the thought of the Deity, and the cowgirls were his disciples. Their circular dances were a ritual of remembrance in which the veils of time and space were flung away.

When Kans learned that two of Devaki's sons walked the Earth, sleepless nights plagued him. To bring matters to a head he convened a tournament and requested the honor of Balaram and Krishna's presence. Gladiators with orders to kill were waiting for them at the arena's gate. With swift maneuvers, the brothers subdued the assassins, rushed the dais, and hurled Kans from his throne.

The people were all moved to sing
When Kans's scepter struck the ground,
For never had they known a king
So diabolically unsound.

Balaram and Krishna restored their grandfather to the throne of Mathura, but a new problem directly arose. Kans's father-in-law, the raja of Magadha, vowed vengeance and commenced a series of aggressions. Years of war followed, finally prompting Krishna to remove the population of his city to a location far from the slings and arrows of their harassers. Beside the Arabian Sea he founded the utopia of Dwarka.

Opprobrium does not accrue
To one who answers force with force,
But neither is dishonor due
To one who takes another course.

Krishna might have lived out his days in easy contentment, but matters fell out otherwise. In Hastinapur, rival bands of cousins known as the Kauravs and Pandavs were locked in a bitter dispute over succession. Krishna attempted mediation, only to be met with sneers from the bumptious Kaurav chief. The scoundrel's mockery ceased when Krishna flashed a glimpse of his eidolon, which resembled lightning.

When battle was imminent, Krishna offered the two parties a choice. They could have his army or his personal presence, albeit unarmed. The Kauravs chose the former, the Pandavs the latter. The Pandavs chose wisely.

Krishna drove the chariot of the Pandav grandee Arjuna. As Arjuna surveyed the serried lines, his face blanched and stomach heaved. Krishna reassured him. "Duty is everything," he said. "Do not fear death; the soul is immortal."

Krishna then revealed himself as the Soul of Souls, unveiling limbs and faces one after another, galaxies beyond number swimming in each pair of eyes. Fear departed Arjuna's heart and Krishna propelled the chariot into the fray.

In no war did more heroes die
Than in the Kurukshetra War.
No end of arrows streaked the sky
And miles were painted red with gore.

For eighteen days the battle raged. In the end, the Pandavs triumphed. In Hastinapur their leader Yudhishthir was crowned king to loud ovations.

Back in Dwarka, with the passing of years Krishna observed his people lapsing in their manners. In spite of his guidance and example, the Yadavs were becoming frivolous, boorish, and generally unpleasant. When the revered sage Narada visited the city, a band of pranksters impertinently made sport of him. Far from amused, Narada pronounced his curse on the entire Yadav clan.

Seeing that his kairos* had reached its end, Krishna retreated to the jungle and awaited death. As he slept nestled among aromatic shrubs, a hunter's arrow struck his foot. At the very moment Krishna's lifeblood poured out of him, a tsunami inundated Dwarka and an age of dissolution began.

Do not bewail the death of one
For whom the body is a shirt;
The soul can never come undone,
Nor does it even suffer hurt.

Hearing of Krishna's demise, Yudhishthir renounced his throne and, in the company of his queen and five brothers, struck out on the perilous path to Mount Meru. A dog attached itself to the pilgrims along the way. As the party progressed through the crags and gorges of the Himalayas, one by one they succumbed to the elements and fell dead. In the end, only Yudhishthir and the dog remained.

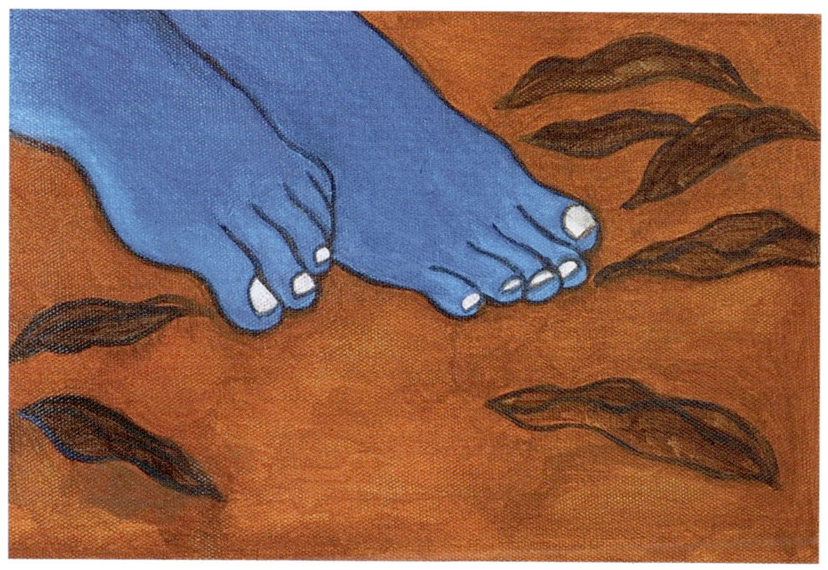

A hunter's arrow struck Krishna's foot.

On the peak of Meru, a radiant angel swung down in a flying car and congratulated Yudhishthir on his success. "Please be seated," the angel said. "I'll convey you to the Garden straight away. Only . . . the dog may not accompany us."

Yudhishthir politely declined, explaining that abandoning the dog was out of the question. The dog looked up with a smile. Its body suddenly altered; it was now Azrael. Forthwith, a host of angels and sages appeared in astral and etheric forms to join the Angel of Death in bestowing benedictions on Yudhishthir. So doing, they ushered him into the car.

A higher life is never found
By casting off a loyal friend,
So bear in mind Yudhishthir's hound
And stay devoted to the end.

Solar Theology

In Egypt, the keepers of mysteries saw changing seasons. The ancient college at Heliopolis continued to preserve the Hurakhshic tradition inaugurated by Ra and Hathor. A second college arose in Hermopolis, dedicated to the teachings of the elusive angel Amen. Some aver that Amen was none other than Ham, son of Noah, speaking from the beyond.

The people of the Nile valley were a mélange born of trade and war. Olive-skinned Japhethites swooped down from the north as merchants one year, marauders the next. Ebon-toned Hamites from Kush in the south figured as tributaries and overlords by turns. As for the bronze Shemites of the east, they became Egypt's shadow, and Egypt became theirs.

The umbra is a place wherein
The disavowed resides concealed
Until, to everyone's chagrin,
It saunters out to stand revealed.

The Shepherd Kings were Jews from the Levant. Some say they ascended the ranks of Egyptian society by dint of sheer merit. Others hold that they seized power as invaders. In either case, after a century of rule they were ousted by Theban votaries of Amen.

The prognosticator Amenophis now entered the stage. A sufferer of unmanageable phobias, he persuaded the pharaoh to evict from the kingdom every person of unsound body. The ill and infirm were accordingly cast out in the desert.

The outcasts refused to die. Led by the Heliopolitan priest Osarsiph, they allied themselves with the banished Shepherd Kings and returned to Egypt in force. For thirteen years they ransacked the temples and palaces of the nation.

Followers of Amen finally drove off the vandals. Amen's cult was bolstered and Hermopolis became the center of sacred power in the kingdom. But the college of Heliopolis endured, and its priests maintained a quiet channel of communication with the wisdom keepers among the Jews. The Heliopolitans and rabbis both remembered Abraham's initiation at the House of Atum.

The prophet Abraham was still
A link between the nations twain,
And Hagar stood for the goodwill
That ought forever to remain.

The Eighteenth Dynasty, a Japhethite line, flourished at Thebes. Gold, precious stones, fragrant aloeswood, and exotic pelts poured into Egypt from its tributaries, Syria, Phoenicia, and Nubia. Under Amenhotep III, the temples of Amen in Karnak and Luxor reached the peak of their glory. The winds, however, were soon to change. The pharaoh's son Amenhotep IV was an initiate of the college of Heliopolis.

Early in his reign, Amenhotep IV raised the hackles of Amen's priests by erecting roofless temples in Karnak. This was just the beginning. The new pharaoh was a zealous illuminationist; his devotion was solely for Aten, the Sun behind the sun.

Amenhotep IV announced that the gods had ceased their movements and should not be relied on. Only the uncreated God, Aten, deserved praise. Assuming the name Akhenaten, "in Service to Aten," the prophet-king disbanded Egypt's priesthoods, quit Thebes, and established a new imperial capital, "Aten's Horizon." With lifted hands, he prayed:

> O living Aten, liege of eternity, you rise in glory. Your love is potent. Your iridescent light beguiles every face. Your dawning rays irradiate the whole of the Earth. Every heart throbs at the sight of you. You shine and every land rejoices. Singers, male and female, chant jubilant hymns in the House of the Benben Stone and the temples of the City of the Horizon. You are the living Disc and eternity is your emanation. You are alone, but your myriad powers give your creatures life; the sight of your rays is their very breath. When you rise, plants unfurl in the desert and buds burst into flower; at the sight of your face, they drink to inebriation. Animals gambol and birds rise from their nests, flap their wings, and soar in circles of praise.

With Akhenaton's death, his heirs abandoned Aten's Horizon in favor of Memphis. In Thebes, the cult of Amen regained its feet. The mystagogues of Heliopolis, however, continued their meditations on the Sun behind the sun, and another revolution impended ahead. In the Diwan, a committee was already at work.

Changing Fortunes

Esau and Jacob were the twin sons of Isaac and his wife Rebecca. They feuded even in the womb; Jacob came out clutching Esau's heel. By recourse to trickery, Jacob obtained the blessing Isaac had intended for Esau. Esau brayed for his brother's blood and Jacob fled.

In Harran, Jacob performed a miracle. By means of a precise sequence of solvative and coagulatory operations, he fused the twelve stones of Adam and Eve's ancient temple into a single massive crystal. Having done this, he laid his head on the stone and slept. In his dream, angels ascended and descended the rungs of a ladder. The Deity then appeared in a flash of illumination. When Jacob awoke, only dust was left of the physical Philosopher's Stone. The stone's numen* now resided in his chest.

A ladder rises through the sky
And culminates before the Throne.
If you would witness God on high,
Internalize the Sophic Stone.

Jacob settled in Hebron. Of his many sons and daughters, his favorite was Joseph. Joseph's brothers resented his preeminence and threw him in a well. Joseph was fortunately rescued; unfortunately, his rescuer was a slave trader.

An old Egyptian tale tells of a certain Bata who lived with

his elder brother, Anubis, and the latter's wife. The wife sought to seduce Bata. When he proved unresponsive, she mendaciously accused him of laying hands on her. A vigilant pair of cows warned Bata that Anubis lay in ambush for him. Bata fled, never to return.

History often repeats itself; at Tanis, the tale recurred. This time, Bata was Joseph. Anubis was his purchaser, Potiphar. The wife was Potiphar's wife, Zulaykha. The result was that Joseph found himself in prison.

The loudest tend to have their way
And truth is trampled on the ground
Until arrives the fateful day
When honest heads at last are crowned.

Joseph knew the meaning of every dream. Word reached the pharaoh, Rayyan, that a peerless oneiromancer* was languishing in jail. Rayyan released Joseph and made him his prime minister. Egypt prospered under Joseph's judicious administration.

Zulaykha was now a widow. For all the trouble she had caused him, the lady had a unique place in Joseph's heart. All was forgiven and the two were married.

Secure in his position, Joseph sent for his kinsfolk—even the treacherous brothers. In this way Jews began migrating to Egypt. They were glad to put distance between themselves and Jerusalem, where Zahhak reigned.

After Joseph's death, circumstances altered. Mus'ab, the succeeding pharaoh, looked askance at the Jews, citing the chaos brought by the Shepherd Kings. Mus'ab's successor, Walid, translated his father's anxieties into policies, drafting a decree demoting the Jews to the status of serfs.

◀ *Asiya taught Moses the traditions of Seth and Norea, Isis and Osiris, Ra and Hathor, and Akhenaten and Nefertiti.*

But that was not enough. The Jews would keep multiplying, and would sooner or later overwhelm their masters; so ran his thoughts. And so he signed a second decree: all newborn Jewish boys must die.

Remain alert and don't regard
Your freedom is a paltry thing,
For those before you struggled hard
That you may freely dance and sing.

Asiya, Walid's wife, was an initiate of the college of Heliopolis and a monotheist. She tried to divert her husband from the path of persecution, but to no avail. The pharaoh's heart was rock-hard.

One day, as Asiya was meditating beside the Nile in the capital Pi-Ramesses, a baby floated downstream in a basket. Moses, she named him. She took the boy to her husband and insisted on adoption. Moses yanked the pharaoh's beard.

Walid had profound misgivings, but Asiya reassured him by placing a ruby and a burning ember on the ground. Gabriel guided Moses's hand toward the ember. He thrust it into his mouth, singeing his tongue. "See, he doesn't know what he is doing. He's harmless!" Asiya declared triumphantly.

Kalim Allah: that was the name*
That Moses, may God bless him, bore,
For though his tongue endured a maim,
His speech was Heaven's perfect roar.

Quietly, Asiya taught her adopted son the traditions of Seth and Norea, Isis and Osiris, Ra and Hathor, and Akhenaten and Nefertiti. Moses absorbed it all.

Visions

Moses was two people at once: an Egyptian prince and a Jew. Behind pharaoh's back, he frequented the Jewish quarter and was on close terms with his blood siblings Maryam and Aaron. How long could he sustain this double life?

Matters came to a head when he saw an Egyptian flaying a Jewish laborer. Moses laid him low and fled to the desert.

The life he knew he'd know no more;
There now could be no going back.
The ruffian lay on the floor;
The choice was flee or mount the rack.

He found himself in Midian, road-weary and parched. Ahead was a well. A band of gruff herdsmen were driving off a party of young shepherdesses. Moses dislodged the brutes and won the esteem of the maidens. That evening he was the guest of their father. Dark of skin and bright of eye, this was the Hamite sheik Jethro.

An attachment quickly formed between Moses and Jethro's daughter Zipporah. Jethro sanctioned the match but required that the fugitive come under his spiritual wing. For his part, Moses was eager to absorb the bedouin's gnosis. The murder of the Egyptian haunted him; he needed purgation.

The medicine he needed most
Was here at hand and his to take,
For in the person of his host
He'd found his destined Sufi sheik.

For forty days and nights Moses intoned the Name of the Deity at the bottom of a dry well. Jethro came at intervals to instruct and reassure him. Moses's terrene body remained in place, but his supramundane form roved far. In the invisible world he found the man he had killed, and succeeded in befriending him. Groping together in the dark, the two discovered a shaft of light. They clambered up it, and found themselves in a transfigured landscape.

For ten years Moses remained in Midian, tending Jethro's sheep and assimilating his teachings. Eventually the time came to seek new pastures. As a parting gift, Jethro presented Moses with an heirloom from Adam, a staff cut from the myrtle of Eden.

The path of Moses and Zipporah took them to Sinai, where they were astonished by the sight of a tree ablaze in flame. Moses went to investigate, and was still more greatly astounded to discover that the flames did not burn the tree's leaves or its white, red, and green fruit. This was the tree sprouted from the seed that Seth received at Eden's gate.

Behold, the seed of paradise
Has sunk its root in Mount Sinai
That it may serve as a device
To transmit light from Adonai.

A disembodied voice instructed Moses to remove his sandals. He obeyed and approached the tree. By meanings conveyed in light and sound, the Deity initiated Moses as a prophet and dispatched him to Egypt with the task of liberating the Jews.

With unshorn feet and downcast glance
The awestruck shepherd neared the tree,
And in the rapture of his trance
Bowed deep before the Deity.

The voice directed Moses to throw down his staff. As the staff struck the ground, a jet of fire shot from the tree and ignited it. The staff shuddered, sprang up, and assumed the form of a serpent. A jolt of electricity surged up Moses's spine; he swiveled. The Deity calmed his nerves. Moses placed his hand on his heart; the hand blanched the color of snow.

Moses duly returned to Egypt. Every jaw at court dropped as he stood before the throne and demanded the freedom of the Jews. To drive home his message, he brandished his staff and held up his white hand.

Walid riposted that he too could command magic. With a signal, his necromancers stepped forward. The magicians tossed phosphorescent powder into a smoldering brazier. Wisps of acrid smoke writhed up, the coils becoming snakes. But Moses's staff was now a serpent as well. Spines surged with voltage, flickering violet traceries adumbrated the wings of multitudinous seraphs, and Moses's dragon swallowed the sorcerers' sooty reptiles one by one.

By means of Musa's serpent-wand
A higher octave was produced,
And by the vision thereby spawned,
A truer knowing was induced.

There followed a dystopian reckoning by turns atmospheric, pandemical, and zoic: darkness, plagues, tainted water, swarms of frogs and locusts. With Moses, Maryam, and Aaron at the fore, the Jews banded together and set out to the east, never to look back. Walid and his legions pursued them as far as the Sea of Qulzum, where they suffered engulfment. In Pi-Ramesses, Daluka, a lady of large perception, was chosen as the succeeding pharaoh.

The migrants, through the duration of their meanderings across the peninsula of Sinai, sustained themselves on manna, a salubrious honey-frost, and slaked their thirst at limpid springs that welled up at the touch of Moses's daimonic staff. Along the way, Moses routinely paused at metal-rich hummocks to mine antimony, cinnabar, verdigris, quicksilver, and other requisites of alchemy. His ensuing operations, assisted by his apprentice, Qarun, yielded abundant quantities of gold.

When the travelers reached Mount Horeb, Moses called for a sojourn. He proceeded to seclude himself on the peak, fast, and recite the Name of the Deity. On the fortieth day, a seething cloud filled the sky. Moses pleaded for a glimpse of the Deity's Face.

Cattle appeared in a crashing stampede, followed by bellowing lions, then screeching eagles. Next there came creatures whose bodies were of burning ice, others like incarnate rainbows, and still others with four faces, each brighter than the sun. Moses heard a voice thunder, "Show him!" Four gigantic angels wheeled the Throne into sight. When Moses looked up, his senses went black.

When Moses stood on Sinai's peak
Desirous of the August Face,
The Deity's intense mystique
Expelled his mind from time and space.

Trials on the Trail

Moses opened his eyes; Gabriel was in front of him. In the archangel's hands were a bundle of lazurite tablets intagliated with revelations. Moses took them, kissed them, pressed them to his eyes. It was time to go down the mountain.

A descent from sky to earth always requires acclimation. But the scene that greeted Moses at the mountain's foot defied all expectations. A figment by the name of Behemoth had taken advantage of Moses's absence to slander him as an absconder. The phantom urged the worship of himself as the only reasonable recourse for the Jews. A good number of Moses's followers tergiversated and were now dancing circles around a golden calf molded to represent their new deliverer.

When Moses came with staff in hand,
Behemoth crept into the shade.
The prophet voiced his reprimand
And all repented having strayed.

It now befell Moses to dispose of the calf. Gold does not easily dissolve; for days Moses applied himself to melting, calcinating, and pulverizing the effigy, until in the end only a fine powder remained. The powder merged into the desert sand and the figment was driven out for good.

When dust returns to Mother Earth
Or water flows into the sea,
The particles obtain rebirth
And wander onward, newly free.

By and by another rebellion broke out. This time the culprit was Qarun. While Moses manufactured gold for the public weal, a different prospect excited the mind of his apprentice. Qarun yearned for aggrandizement. He secretly duplicated Moses's procedures and spent the yield on an army of henchmen. As soon as he launched his coup, however, the Diwan thwarted him and that was the end of it.

When wealth is spent to nurture power
And power is plied to nourish wealth,
Expect a harvest duly sour
And ruinous to human health.

When order was restored, Moses took a leave of absence. With the stalwart Joshua by his side, he traveled to a place where two waters mingled. Khizr, the Green Man, was waiting for them. Moses gave Joshua leave to return to the tribes, and seated himself at Khizr's feet.

The immortal sage accepted Moses's discipleship but stipulated that there be no questions. It fell out, however, that despite his best intentions Moses was unable to suppress his astonishment in the face of Khizr's strange doings. Khizr finally explained himself and sent Moses off with a farewell benediction.

To speak is intellectual,
But silent stillness is an art.

Discourse may be effectual,
But quietude befits the heart.

Further adventures remained for the migrants. They solved mysteries, battled tyrants, contended with belligerent orionids, and navigated fantastical landscapes. When their spirits sank, Maryam roused them with the rhythms of her timbrel. At the head of their caravan went the tent known as the Tabernacle. Within it stood the Ark of the Covenant, the glowing box of acacia wood in which the Tablets rested.

In the end, the Jews reached the Holy Land they had so long sought. They were a stone's throw away when Moses halted the procession. He excused himself and approached a ruddy dune standing hard by.

Angels were digging a grave. Moses expressed his admiration. They asked if he would like to rest there. He replied that indeed he would, and lowered himself into the recess. He turned his thoughts to the Deity and his soul left his body.

When following the desert trail
That leads from homelessness to home,
Find joy in every hill and vale,
For God created you to roam.

The Folk of Danu

Since time out of mind, a colossal oak called Bile has kept watch over the southern edge of the Black Forest of Rum. The oak has seen droughts, floods, and fires, and still it endures. Beside the oak, a crystal spring known as Danu gurgles. The water of the spring flows eastward, mingling with other rills to become the Danube River, which issues ultimately into the Black Sea in Thracia.

One day, two orionids happened to visit the spring for refreshment at the same moment, a man and a woman. The man was The Dagda, a sturdy young buck with knowing eyes. The woman was Brigid, a savant equally expert in the literary and healing arts. Frosty greetings led to thawing words and, finally, the sizzling resolution to meet again. The two continued their trysts beside the spring, and before the season was out The Dagda and Brigid had joined their lives.

Beside the oak and bubbling source,
Between the woman and the man,
Transpired an attractive force
Engendering a faerie clan.

The oak was a favorite haunt of Azrael, and the angel Ardvisura frequented the waters of the spring. These two numinaries became the preceptors of Brigid and The Dagda. The name Bile seemed too holy to utter, so the pair called the oak Draoi. With the passage of time, adepts of Azrael's sacred science came to be known as "draoids," or Druids. The children of Brigid and The Dagda were named for the spring: Tuatha Dé Danann, the folk of Danu.

When Azrael and Ardvisura were satisfied with the Tuatha Dé Danann's competence in matters shamanic they sent them north for further study under the third Votan's heirs in Thule. The Odinic college had chapters in four cities of perpetual winter: Falias, Gorias, Finias, and Murias. The Tuatha Dé Danann spent long years moving between these institutions and assimilating their mysteries. Upon graduation, the Thulean hierologists awarded the clan four magical treasures: a monolith, a spear, a sword, and a cauldron.

Azrael and Ardvisura now appeared to the Tuatha Dé Danann to propose next steps. They advised the clan to proceed to a verdant island south of Thule and west of the Black Forest, the name of which was Erin. This enchanted isle was to be their homeland forever after.

And so the faes went forth by sea
To settle on an emerald shore
Where ponies frisk upon the lea
And, in snug hollows, badgers snore.

Erin

The Tuatha Dé Danann were not the first to settle in Erin and would not be the last. The original people of the isle were a nation of tempestuous elementals known as Fomors. They subsist to this day, lodged in reefy strongholds at the bottom of the sea. I hasten to add that Fomors are amphibious and by no means waterbound.

Sightings are rare but not unheard of. Some Fomors resemble ambling piles of barnacled pumice while others display a nacreous sleekness. Only rarely have nonelementals won their good graces.

Beware the jagged stony shoals
And shun the darkling caverns deep;
Be leery of ill-willie trolls
And all who roam while humans sleep.

Well before the Flood, Noah sensed catastrophe ahead. He alerted his granddaughter Cessair and she took his hint to heart. Cessair roused her friends and fled with them in a trio of ships. Two capsized, but the barque piloted by Cessair reached Erin intact. Cessair's shipmates were her confidantes Alba, German, Espa, Triage, and Gothiam; the seer Fintan mac Bóchra was also given a berth. Soon after landing, Cessair's five friends set out in various directions. These adventurers would become the grandmothers of the British, German, Spanish, Thracian, and Gothic people.

Fintan remained and married Cessair. When the Flood struck Erin, both were drowned, along with their children. Cessair and the youngsters traveled on to the stars, but Fintan had methodically reinforced his diaphane and survived terrestrially by means of it. Sometimes Fintan's ethereality was andromorphic, but just as often he appeared as a salmon or hawk. Like Khizr he lived for centuries and applied himself to guiding those perceptive enough to seek his counsel. "The Salmon of Knowledge" became his sobriquet.

In all of human history
Few personages can compare
With Fintan, man of mystery,
And with the mariner Cessair.

Three hundred years after the Flood, another company of migrants reached Erin. These were the People of Partholon, whose roots lay in Anatolia. They tended cattle, planted fields, and coaxed the landscape to produce four plains and seven lakes. The Fomors constantly harried them, but this was not the cause of their downfall; their demise, when it occurred, was caused by a plague. The only survivor was Tuan mac Cairill, who endured etherically in the manner of his mentor, Fintan mac Bóchra.

Another wave of migrants soon followed. These were the People of Nemed, expatriates of the Caspian coast. By their efforts, twelve more plains and four new lakes came into being. Like the Partholonians, the Nemedians found themselves perpetually at war with the Fomors. Unlike their predecessors, however, they failed to withstand the elementals' depredations, and perished en masse at their hands.

Only a small contingent of Nemedians survived. Half of these took refuge on the nearby island of Albion and merged with Alba's descendants. The other portion fled to Yunan,* where they were cruelly enslaved and made to haul clay and rock in gunnysacks. In this way they came to be known as "Firbolg," Men of the Bags.

The Firbolg eventually escaped Yunan and returned to Erin. They were a mellower people now. Among other realizations, the Firbolg had come to see the necessity of establishing good relations with the primordials of the land they wished to inhabit. In Erin, this meant making peace with the Fomors. The Firbolg did just that, and flourished.

Just why is it so hard to see
That to the Ancient Ones is due
A nod to their priority
Before enacting something new?

Houses at War

The Tuatha Dé Danann arrived in a purple cloud. They surveyed the knolls and dingles spread out before them and dreamt euphoric dreams. The gorse-combed breeze of Erin was good to breathe.

But who were the figures approaching with speed? A Firbolg delegation drew up and, with wary words and still warier looks, parleyed with the new arrivals. For their part, the Dannids were genial but firm. They had come to stay, they announced, and would require half the island. The Firbolg were not pleased.

Though both were people of good heart
And intimate with wisdom's ways,
They failed to make a friendly start
And thus were doomed to painful days.

War ensued and, though both armies conducted themselves with unimpeachable chivalry, casualties were numerous. Eochaid, king of the Firbolg, was slain, and Nuada, king of the Tuatha Dé Danann, lost his right hand. In the end, the Firbolg were dispersed.

A double conundrum now bedeviled the Tuatha Dé Danann. The first problem was that Nuada could no longer be king on account of his missing hand. The second was that, by displacing the Firbolg, the Tuatha Dé Danann had offended the Fomors. The only solution, they concluded, was to invite the heir of the King under the Sea, Bres, son of Elathan, to mount the throne of Tara, their new capital, and rule them.

The Tuatha Dé Danann would come to repent their rashness as Bres revealed himself as an insufferable tyrant. Every year saw him levy a new tax, each more outrageous than the last, and this continued for decades.

Finally, a recourse presented itself. The healer Miach miraculously restored Nuada's hand, requalifying him to rule.

Perhaps it seems that all is lost,
But never should one give up hope,
For nothing ever can exhaust
The length of Allah's saving rope.

Seizing the moment, the Tuatha Dé Danann excused themselves from Bres's patronage and acclaimed Nuada their true and natural liege. The Fomors were predictably outraged, and war followed.

It was just then that Lugh turned up at Tara. Lugh was a Fomor by maternal descent but Dannite on his father's side. He said there was no art, science, magical craft, or martial discipline he had not mastered to a degree never before seen. The ministers of court put him to the test and, indeed, he had spoken factually.

The Tuatha Dé Danann were thrilled to have such a prodigy in their camp and feared to lose him. Nuada sent every spear-bearing arm to the frontline but kept Lugh back.

The decisive battle was fought on Samhain, the day of the dead. The carnage was overwhelming. Seeing Nuada fall, Lugh took to the field. An aisle opened between him and Balor of the One Eye, the grimmest of the Fomors. To look into Balor's eye was certain death, and the cyclops was now ogling Lugh. With downcast gaze, Lugh hurled a stone and struck out the evil eye. As the malevolent orb rolled on the ground, whole ranks of Fomors perished at the sight of it. The remnant fled in panic.

The optic organ has a power
Transcending its material;
A glance may cause an herb to flower
Or blight a crop of cereal.

The Tuatha Dé Danann were triumphant. But let's pause here to examine another place and time.

Stymied by intractable enemies, a Scythian khan named Finyus Farsa led his horde off the Asiatic steppe and enlisted in the service of the pharaoh Rayyan. Farsa's son Niyul married Rayyan's daughter Scota, who gave birth to a boy named Goidel. All went well for a time, but with the accessions of Musʿab and Walid, the climate in Egypt soured. Refusing to take part in the persecution of the Jews, Farsa's house packed and departed. For four hundred and forty years they roamed the undulating dunes of the Sahara, the narrow passes of the Atlas, and the broad plains of Iberia.

On the Galician littoral, Breogán, now leader of the tribe, built a fleet of ships and a lofty lighthouse. On a clear winter evening, from the top of the tower, Breogán's son Ith clairvoyantly spied Erin. His head swam with visions of golden apples, and he set out immediately.

Ith arrived at Tara at an awkward moment. The funeral obsequies of Nuada had just concluded, and three claimants to the throne were locked in disagreement. Lacking a better idea, they consulted Ith. Ith had little to advise but much to say about the lush fecundity of Erin. Ith's panegyric aroused their suspicions and they villainously took his life.

Poor Ith! He lacked all sense of tact
And made it clear he craved their land.
For this offense he was attacked;
Such was their violent reprimand.

Ith's nephew Milé swore revenge, and crossed the sea with a brave company. As Milé's ships neared the shore, the Druid of the band, Amergin, sang a hymn to the Deity, and a great wind filled their sails. In Tara, the Milesians and the Tuatha Dé Danann agreed that combat should proceed and the winner should have Erin. Two terrible battles were fought, and the Milesians prevailed.

As the Fomors had retreated before the Tuatha Dé Danann, the Dannites now ceded the island's surface to the Milesians and withdrew underground. To this day, a tumulus in Erin can only mean one thing: beneath it stands a well-appointed hall housing a family of faes, or "sidhe" as they are commonly called.

And what became of Lugh? Diminished in size and strength, but still exemplary in gnosis, Lugh Chromain is now known as Leprechaun.

And should you spot Sir Leprechaun
I urge you, kindly spare a thought
For those who live beneath the lawn
And all the splendor that they've wrought.

Westering

The Phoenicians of Byblos never forgot how Isis had served as a nursemaid to their royal house, or how Osiris had slept in one of the palace pillars. Like a watchful younger sibling they studied the ways of the Egyptians but carefully refrained from imitating them outright. Impressed but not altogether satisfied with Kemet's hieroglyphs, they recast the strange icons in the tidier form of alphabetic letters.

The animals were good and well,
But Byblos sought a sleeker script;
It wished, at last, to break the spell
And rescue logic from its crypt.

With a tip of the hat to the picturesque barges of the Egyptians, the Phoenicians proceeded to erect a fleet of ships the likes of which the world had never seen. Some have it that these galleys, heavy with murex, sailed as far as Hesperidia. More often they landed on the Nile delta or the shores of Crete.

If Egypt was Phoenicia's elder sister, Crete was her twin. Both nations prized the brine of the White Sea as the very blood of their blood. When Amorites sacked Byblos, droves of Phoenicians sailed to Crete to rebuild their fortunes in Knossos or a nearby town.

In former times the island had offered haven to refugees from Atlantis. The Atlanteans brought with them their two leading cults, the mysteries of the bull and those of the snake. The bull cult concerned itself with the wisdom of the sun; the snake cult delved into the gnosis of the earth.

The bellowings of bulls were fraught
With intimations from Old Sol,
And serpents by their hissings taught
Chthonic pathways to the Goal.

The most ardent votary of the bull cult in Knossos was a young bashaw named Asterion. Asterion's ample means enabled him to extend lavish hospitality to the migrants pouring in from Phoenicia, and he drank with them late into the night. In this way he learned of Princess Europa, who still lived in the palace of Byblos, pitiable though the condition of the city was.

Europa's name now haunted him
And life without her held no cheer.
This was no mere romantic whim;
He'd know no rest till she was near.

It was Europa's habit to watch the sun set over the White Sea. Her name, her grandmother had told her, meant "west." She secretly longed to follow the sun over the rippling horizon. One evening the magenta luster attending the sun's subsidence was of such a burning intensity it seemed as though the veil between worlds had been momentarily drawn back.

A Cretan vessel now appeared,
Its sails awash in mauvy rays,

And as it gradually neared
It seemed to concentrate the blaze.

Europa stood motionless as the sloop pulled up to the pier. A bronze bull gleamed from its prow. Above the figurehead, a young man's visage came into view. It was a familiar face; she knew its lineaments from unforgettable dreams.

Asterion debarked, greeted Europa with spellbound eyes, and inquired if she wished to sail away with him. She replied in the affirmative and they set out at once.

The land of Europe gained its name
The moment when the torch was passed
And Asia's night-illuming flame
Became Minoa's protoplast.

The Labyrinth

Europa's brother Cadmus solemnly pledged to rescue her. Not knowing where to look, he found himself drawn to the island Samothrace, where the traditions of the Kabiri still thrived. The heirs of the Kabiri initiated him and introduced him to fellow initiate Harmonia, whom he espoused. When the nuptials were solemnized, the Kabiri heirs sent the pair to Delphi.

The Pythia of Delphi syncretized the Atlantean serpent sect with the legacy of the Hyperborean shaman Apollo. She instructed Cadmus and Harmonia in the method of waking the coil in the coccyx. The Pythia absolved Cadmus of his brotherly mission, assuring him that Europa needed no saving. Instead, she said, Cadmus and Harmonia should follow a wandering heifer and lay the founding stone of a new city on the spot at which it halted.

Be guided by an ambling cow:
Thus counseled the sagacious crone.
They did just as she said and now
They knew just where to place the stone.

◀ *Minos expanded the vaults under his palace to create a sprawling subterranean labyrinth.*

In this way the great metropolis of Thebes was founded.

One further accomplishment must be credited to Cadmus. He, a Phoenician by birth and education, invented the Greek script.

In the end, the poets say, Cadmus and Harmonia were transformed into snakes. What they mean, of course, is that the pair perfected the art of moving subtle breath up and down their spines.

A myth can never be unlocked
Without the necessary key;
The visionary path is blocked
To those who lack the eyes to see.

The Pythia was, of course, correct with respect to Europa: she required no rescue. She was perfectly content in Knossos. She had reached the Occident of her dreams.

Minos, son of Europa and Asterion, was a born leader. As master shipwright of Knossos, he oversaw the building of a breathtaking fleet of galleys. This achieved, he set his mind to the ordering of society, and drafted the first legal code known to Rum. Old feuds were settled, trade boomed, roads were cobbled, olive trees multiplied, and the citizens of Crete unanimously hailed Minos as their king.

The people did not hesitate
To crown the shipwright as their shah.
In fact, they rushed to coronate
This bringer of respected law.

Minos's queen consort was the orionid sibyl Pasiphaë, sister of the famous enchantress Circe. Minos and Pasiphaë named their son after Minos's father, and entrusted the boy to his instruction. Under Asterion's tutelage, Asterion II grew to become a brilliant mystagogue of the cult of the bull. His sacerdotal name was Minotaur.

Minos expanded the vaults under his palace to create a sprawling subterranean labyrinth. On specified holy days, Asterion II took his place at the center of the maze. One by one, mystai groped through the dark passageways. As their bodies moved through the architectural puzzle, their astral forms navigated the planets of the solar system. In the end, they reached Minotaur. Behind his eyes were the eyes of Hurakhsh, and behind the gaze of the sun-angel was the perfect light of the Deity.

The poets say that no one returned from the labyrinth alive; Minotaur slew them all. They mean, as every gnostic knows, that the mystai underwent an initiatic death and resurrection. Their faded old selves disintegrated, and they emerged reborn and shining.

Asterion has been maligned;
He never hurt a single soul.
He was a doctor of the mind
Who made the fragmentary whole.

Minos and Asterion II were succeeded by a long line of Minoses and Minotaurs. Knossos was the envied pearl of the White Sea. Then one day catastrophe struck. A volcano on the nearby islet of Thera erupted, sending cataclysmic breakers into the harbor of Knossos. The city incurred serious damage and the labyrinth collapsed entirely. Afterward, Crete was never the same.

The Muse's Son

There was no end to the rejoicing in Thrace when Oeagrus wedded Calliope, the Chief of all Muses. It was as if the king had married Music itself. Spines tingled when Calliope sang, and she sang all the more sweetly after Orpheus's birth. Feeling as though he had done his part, Oeagrus joined Dionysius's expedition to India, leaving Calliope to raise the boy on her own.

The prince's mother's milk was song
And never was there better cream;
The Muse's lullabies were long
And sweet as an elysian dream.

Orpheus was unquestionably his mother's son. When he played his lyre, the branches of the trees quivered in consonance and whole flocks of birds congregated to listen. He had no taste for profane airs; his repertoire consisted entirely of paeans to the angels he encountered while walking in the Odrysian mountains.

When Orpheus intoned the names
Of angels bright and swift of wing,
The nymphs all quit their jaunty games
To sit and listen to him sing.

Following Oeagrus's return from India, Orpheus kissed the hands of his parents and set out on his own sortie. A fleet skiff took him across the White Sea and up the Nile. Finding himself in Pi-Ramesses, he thought it proper to pay his respects at Walid's court.

As Orpheus presented his credentials at the gate, strange prismatic lights flashed from the interior. Orpheus watched in awe as an Olympian figure emerged, his eyes livid with righteous wrath, a serpent writhing in his blanched right hand.

He'd seen the prophet of the age,
The knower of the Royal Art,
And naught on Earth could now assuage
The yearning that beset his heart.

Orpheus succeeded in gaining admittance as Moses's disciple and sat at his feet for the full term of the prophet's stay at the capital. The association produced a new richness in the baritone of his voice. When the plagues arrived and the Jews hurried to depart Egypt, Moses blessed Orpheus and sent him north again, intimating that he was needed in Aeolia.

Orpheus reached Aeolia just in time to join Jason and his intrepid crew as they boarded Jason's galley, the Argo, for an adventure that would be remembered forever after. With Atalanta, Heracles, Theseus, and now Orpheus lending their talents, the Argonauts were a uniquely competent squad. Their objective was to obtain the fabled relic known as the Golden Fleece, enabling Jason to claim his rightful throne.

The Golden Fleece was many things: a wooly gleam, a seraphic animal, a carnose idea, a squared circle, a pulsing piece of Azoth. Put succinctly, it was a Philosopher's Stone capable of transmuting lead into gold.

The Golden Fleece was many things, capable of transmuting lead into gold.

Just as the Argonauts set out
To win the lustrous Golden Fleece,
So must we all pursue the route
That leads to everlasting peace.

The Argo's passage from Aeolia to Colchis on the Black Sea, where the Golden Fleece hung on an ancient oak, was a long and winding one. At each turn, Orpheus's strings ensured success. His strains attracted propitious winds, calmed rough waters, and, at the crucial moment, enchanted the serpent that guarded the alchemical pelt.

Beware—do not rush out headlong;
If you would gain the golden fur,
You must be furnished with a song
Able to make a dragon purr.

The quest was complete. With Jason established on his throne, Orpheus allowed himself the privilege of lovemaking. There was an orionid lass he had always admired, Eurydice by name, and he now courted her in earnest. She assented to his suit, and the two were married.

Alas, soon after the nuptials, Eurydice succumbed to a viper bite.

Orpheus could not let her go. With eyes rolled back in bakshic* trance, he extracted his astral essence from the casing of its terrene form and pursued his bride through the mazy catacombs of Malakut.

By recourse to a sequence of ingenious musical interventions he managed to navigate the deadfalls, guard dogs, and naysayers of the netherworld. Presently he reached the asphodel meadow in which Eurydice loitered.

Orpheus wailed a plangent, ululating invocation of the Name of the Deity in a melodic mode never heard before or since. The wildflowers parted to make a path, Eurydice ran to him, and the pair departed the world of the dead together.

The Orphics, to this very day,
Are known to carry in their sack
A golden passport, so that they
Can visit Hades and come back.

The Temple

Though Moses was not fated to enter the Promised Land, his followers did enjoy that happy fate. Joshua led them as they exuberantly toured the rolling tracts of milk and honey that lay ahead.

For forty years they'd known no rest,
And now, at last, they felt at home.
They longed to build a padded nest
And know the meaning of shalom.

The tableau that met their gaze, however, was by no means empty of human figures. Between Gilead and Dan, a medley of groups cooperated, competed, and clashed, among them descendants of Palestinos; Shemite Edomites, Ammonites, Moabites, Amalekites, and Arameans; and Hamite Jebusites and Amorites. Joshua's caravan was alternately welcomed with courtesy and ruthlessly assaulted. Through the hail of flowers and stones they made their way.

After Joshua, a succession of judges adjudicated the disputes of the Jews and directed their war parties. The arrangement was less than satisfactory, leading the seer Samuel to conceive the necessity of a king. When a young man named Saul appeared before him looking for lost donkeys, Samuel anointed him.

Such is the way of history;
The unexpected comes to pass.
Causation is a mystery;
A king is crowned thanks to an ass.

Samuel likewise anointed Saul's successor, David. In David, the Jews had found a monarch with eyes afire with transmundane vision. He played intricate maqams on the harp, sent up impassioned orisons to the Deity, and busied himself with plans for the raising of an epochal temple in Jerusalem. But his reign was fraught with war, and when the day of his death came, the temple remained unbuilt.

Not every dream will be fulfilled
While staying as the planet's guest,
Yet all that is divinely willed
In proper course will manifest.

Solomon ruled after David, and oversaw an age of consummate peace. The wisdom for which he was famed was a gift from Heaven. In a dream the Deity appeared and inquired if he desired a boon. Longevity or the chastisement of his foes were the last things on his mind. He asked for an understanding heart, and it was given to him.

Request of God a heart that knows
And feels all that it's meant to feel,
For as a heart awakes and grows
It gains the power to bless and heal.

Snips of conversations no one else could hear reached Solomon on the breeze. In fact, he was able to make out thoughts as well as words.

The prophet-king's favorite pastime was to roam the lanes of Jerusalem incognito. He found himself repeatedly drawn to a field on the outskirts of the city. The breeze informed him that it was jointly owned by two brothers: one a bachelor of modest means and the other a prosperous family man.

At summer's end, Solomon saw that the brothers had divided their harvest in two heaping stooks, one for each. On a certain evening Solomon watched the indigent brother furtively transfer a sizable portion of his stack to the pile of his sibling, mumbling, "He has so many mouths to feed." And what should occur the following evening but the same event in reverse: the well-to-do brother shifted half of his grain to the other stook, muttering, "His is the greater need."

Solomon had been looking for a suitable piece of land on which to build the temple his father had left unrealized. Even ground, good drainage, and congenial surroundings had been the considerations foremost in his mind. But here before him was something vastly more vital: a stirring human reflection of the Deity's generosity.

Solomon paid the brothers a princely price, acquired the field, and commenced construction.

The Temple's sacred quality
Consists of love and nothing more.
Why dawdle in frivolity
When every moment is a door?

Hiram of Tyre sent cedar and limestone from Phoenicia, as well as a master builder, also named Hiram. The elementals and orionids of the court mined the countryside for gold and precious stones. For seven years the work went on.

Finally the gates were flung open. An orchestra made a jubilant din as priests conducted the Ark of the Covenant from the turbulence of the courtyard, where a sacrificial fire belched clouds of acrid smoke, into the incense-sweetened air of the temple. The priests proceeded to carry the Ark past gold-paneled walls, up steep stone steps, and through a curtain of orange and purple linen. They lowered their load in the consecrated cube of the Holy of Holies, where Moses's tablets would rest between two massive ormulu cherubs.

Solomon then declared for all to hear that this would be a house of prayer for Israel and all nations.

And so it was until, four centuries later, Nebuchadnezzar breached Jerusalem's defenses, ransacked the Temple, and dragged the Jews off to captivity in Babylon.

The Hoopoe Plays Cupid

And what became of the Ark of the Covenant? There hangs a tale, Mir Abu'l-Qasim.

Because Solomon had asked for, and received, an understanding heart, he was endowed with a unique qualification: he could understand the speech of the birds and the ants.

If all of us, in every clime,
Could speak with every beast and bird,
Imagine how we'd sagely chime
In consonance with all we heard.

Once, in a moment of distraction, Solomon brusquely brushed an ant off his sleeve. From the ground the ant hollered, "Why this insufferable heavy-handedness? I serve the same Deity as you." Solomon fell into a swoon. When he woke up he called for the ant, and his attendants ushered her in. "Forgive me," he said softly. The ant replied, "I will—on the condition that you desist from grasping at the world, keep your appetites in check, and show generosity to those who request your assistance." Solomon solemnly made the required pledge and the ant absolved him.

◀ *Solomon, Bilqis, and the hoopoe Ya'fur*

Do not look haughtily askant
At creatures you don't understand,
For even a defenseless ant
May wield a mighty reprimand.

On another occasion, a lark laid her eggs on the trail along which Solomon and his retinue were marching. The lark's mate objected that she had needlessly endangered their offspring. The mother retorted that Solomon was too considerate to trample a clutch of eggs.

Solomon heard the conversation and sent his chancellor, a wise and dutiful orionid, to stand guard over the nest while the procession passed. Afterward the mother lark chirruped, "Wasn't I right?" Her spouse conceded the point, and added, "I have a locust; I will present it to the king." The mother lark replied, "I have a date; our tribute will be twofold."

The pair then flew to Solomon's palace, laid their gifts before his throne, and humbly prostrated. Solomon said a prayer and affectionately tousled the feathers of their heads. This is the reason larks have tufts on their crowns.

There is a whorl on every head,
A fontanelle of gyrous pores.
Out through this hatch, or so it's said,
The Heaven-going spirit soars.

Birds of many feathers waited upon Solomon. His favorite was a hoopoe named Ya'fur. When Solomon traveled, Ya'fur would fly ahead of the royal cortege to locate hidden springs along the route. Ya'fur's vision penetrated the earth's crust as effortlessly as ordinary eyes gaze through limpid air.

If living water's what you seek,
The hoopoe is, indeed, your bird.
Refrain, therefore, from crass critique
And harken to his every word.

One day Solomon looked for Ya'fur at court only to find him absent without leave. In a fury, the king uttered dire threats. Just then, the hoopoe alighted breathlessly. His excuse, tendered with due punctilio, was this: in Sheba he had discovered a queen of matchless virtue. The delay occurred only because he wished to obtain information that the king might appreciate.

All was forgiven and Solomon dispatched the hoopoe to convey his invitation to the queen forthwith.

He had to find this precious pearl;
Ya'fur did well to point her out.
His thoughts were churning in a whirl;
Their souls were linked, he had no doubt.

Ya'fur fulfilled his mission with alacrity, and the Queen of Sheba, moved by a fascination she could hardly account for, mobilized her court at once.

Bilqis was her name. Half-human and half-jinn, she seemed to live simultaneously in the visible and invisible worlds. Her acumen was legendary, and Solomon felt the full brunt of it when she made short work of the riddles by which he attempted to confound her on their first meeting.

Even so, one of Solomon's ruses struck its mark. Or was the Queen of Sheba merely playing along? Only God knows. In anticipation of her visit, Solomon had slyly paved his throne room with glass, giving the floor the appearance of water. To save her hem from saturation, Bilqis lifted her skirt slightly as she stepped into the chamber, and Solomon triumphantly stole a glimpse of her shapely ankles.

He wanted her to fear to wet
Her hem as he looked on with glee,
And so did things fall out, and yet
His heart, thereby, fell in love's sea.

The attraction between the two monarchs was mutual and fervent. Betrothal was swiftly realized, and the pair spent blissful days and nights together.

Bilqis was prone to visions. In this way she saw that, centuries in the future, an heir of Solomon and herself—in fact, the last of their Western line—would require a ship to fulfill an extraordinary destiny. At her behest, Solomon built a vessel of sufficient durability to last the full length of two millennia. She instructed him to furnish it with a bed, with his father's sword at the baseboard and his own crown at the headboard. She further required him to locate the tree that had burned smokelessly before Moses, and cut three of its branches: one white, one red, and one green. From these branches she had spindles carved and mounted over the bed. When the ship was complete, Bilqis and Solomon watched a host of diaphanous figures descend from the sky in procession as an easterly wind filled the ship's sails, sending it gliding away.

The Queen of Sheba looked ahead
And saw the coming of a knight
Destined to lie in such a bed
En route to realms of sheerest light.

In due course duty called Bilqis back to Yemen. She carried Solomon's seed in her womb.

Twenty-two years later, the couple's son, Menelik, presented himself in Jerusalem. Solomon urged him to stay for good and succeed him as king, but Menelik had only come to pay his respects and was intent on returning to Sheba. Solomon sent him back with an entourage consisting of the foremost lordlings of the land.

Though they held Menelik in appropriate esteem, the lordlings resented their exile. To signal their annoyance they smuggled the Ark of the Covenant out of the Temple and carried it to Sheba. In the long view, it was all for the best, since the theft saved the Ark from the destruction that would eventually engulf the Temple.

The Ark now rests in Aksum in the custodianship of the Abyssinian Church.

The Cow's Lament

Please do not doze, Mir Abu'l-Qasim. We're coming to a subject that may be of particular interest to you.

As we both know, the best parts of your estimable *Book of Kings* derive from our late-night confabulations. But when it came to introducing Zarathustra, you veered off and quoted Daqiqi! Didn't it occur to you to consult me? Never mind; it's in the past. But let me say a word or two about the prophet of light.

On a breezy, sunlit bluff in Scythia a cow chewed her cud. In the torpor of her contentment, her intellect fell into a languid fugue. She blinked, and suddenly another mind looked out from her eyes. A mind of immense proportions and intense perceptions: Earth's own living, breathing psyche.

Commandeering the cow's eidolon, Earth sent it galloping to the Basilica of the Diwan on the slope of Mount Qaf.

The Earth became a comely cow:
What better way to plead her case?
For, let me ask you here and now,
Does there exist a gentler face?

The Earth-cow stood before the assembled prophets and sages, stamped her hooves, and bellowed an anguished lament to the Deity. She complained of ill treatment on every side and begged for a competent protector. A graceful voice answered with the promise that Zarathustra would soon be sent.

When Freno gave birth to Dukdak, a light descended from the heaven of the angels to the realm of the jinns, becoming a figure of fire. When Dukdak conceived Zarathustra, the fiery imago localized itself in the embryo that would eventually assume the physical shape of the Scythian prophet.

The source of everything is bright:
All beings precipitate from light.
Above we basked, but here we fight
To set affairs on Earth aright.

A figment known as Ahriman had long plagued the world. When Ahriman learned of Zarathustra's birth, he insinuated in the minds of the local warlocks the idea that the child must be exterminated at all costs. They made every effort, but the Diwan checked them at each turn.

Dismissing Heaven's guiding hand
Will always prove a sad mistake,
For let the angels merely land
And devils near and far will quake.

On reaching the age of thirty, while celebrating the festival of spring, Zarathustra waded deep in the Jayhun River, leaving only his head dry. On the bank, Gabriel appeared. The archangel astrally summoned Zarathustra to the Basilica of the Diwan, where the Great Epiphany* of the Deity was unveiled to him. The vision shattered and recreated him. To worship and serve the Light of Lights was all that mattered now.

The Face of God had been revealed
And nothing could compare to it.
The call was clear, his fate was sealed,
The candle of his life was lit.

Zarathustra carried the benediction of the Absolute. It remained for him to make common cause with the angels that guard creation. For a decade he climbed windswept crags, bathed under rushing cataracts, and secluded himself in unvisited grottoes.

One by one, six magnificent Species-Sovereigns revealed themselves. Seeing the corona of holy sanction crowning Zarathustra's head, they entrusted him with the care of animals, fires, metals, tracts of land, bodies of water, and the green beings of the Earth.

If you would serve the One-in-All
Then serve all that the One has made,
For everything, however small,
Belongs to Light's endless parade.

The time to preach and teach had now come. With staff in hand, Zarathustra set out for Balkh.

At the court of Gushtasp, Persia's shah of shahs, Zarathustra made an indelible first impression. He opened his palm to reveal a flickering flame. To show that it was harmless, he passed it into the hand of the king, where it continued to painlessly burn.

Gushtasp was enchanted, but the Median philosophers in his train—the magi—glowered in contempt. With the king's permission, they assailed Zarathustra with a barrage of abstruse questions. To their chagrin, he dispelled every enigma with brio.

He cut through all their sophistry
With simple words, straight to the point.
He made things clear as clear can be
And left his critics out of joint.

Gushtasp and his family quickly embraced Zarathustra's religion. The magi too came around in the end. In fact, they did more: they zealously assumed the function of priests of the new faith.

Zarathustra composed a book of sacred songs entitled the Gathas. It wasn't long before these hymns were on the lips of every farmer, merchant, and soldier from the Caucasus to the Hindu Kush.

The prophet of light departed the world at the age of forty-seven, his mission having been accomplished. In Balkh, his daughters, Freno and Srito, continued his work.

Three magi carried the prophet's message to Yunan: Ostanes, Hystaspes, and Zoroaster. A Brahmin named Changranghacha bore the faith to India, and a trickle of adventurous magi trailed after him. These evangelists found themselves in congenial company among India's devotees of Hurakhsh, of which there were many.

The faith of light spread far and wide,
Displacing Ahriman's dark sway.
There'd been a turning of the tide,
And truthfulness had won the day.

The Music of the Spheres

No one who dies really dies. The deceased live on in Malakut and Jabarut. As I'm sure you are aware, Mir Abu'l-Qasim, I am in Malakut as we speak.

Do not suppose the world is flat;
I bid you, dig beneath the crust.
The soul's authentic habitat
Consists of light no less than dust.

Mention has been made of the Argonauts and their quest for the Golden Fleece. The one who spoke for them in all official matters was the savant Aethalides. Following his terrestrial death, Aethalides became, in Malakut, the teacher of a soul newly descended from Jabarut. That soul in due course incarnated as the Turanian hero Euphorbus, who was, alas, slain by Menelaus in the Battle of Troy.

Installed again in Malakut, Euphorbus extended his wing over a descending soul who was to eventually assume corporeality as the Ionian philosopher Hermotimus. It was the practice of Hermotimus to lie on his back, close his eyes, and float to Jabarut. One day, as he was engaged in this exercise, assassins broke in and took his life.

Of course, they took only his life of flesh and blood; he lived on in the jinnic world. There he became the mentor of a soul recently arrived from the angelic heavens. When the proper day came, Hermotimus pronounced his valedictory blessing, and the soul swooped down to Earth, becoming Pythagoras.

Yes, first there was the diplomat,
And then arrived the champion;
Next came the mystic on his mat,
And finally the Samian.

Born in Sidon to parents native to Samos, Pythagoras was a traveler from the very beginning. Following a sojourn in Syria, his parents brought him back to their island and saw that he received the best possible education.

As a young man, the rise of the tyrant Polycrates prompted Pythagoras to quit Samos and continue his education elsewhere. He studied with Pherecydes in Syros and with Thales and Anaximander in Ionia. Thales urged him to make his way to Egypt, and so he did.

Pythagoras lived for a period among the priests of Memphis, digesting the geometrical subtleties of Kemet's ancient monuments. He then journeyed to Byblos and Tyre, where he mingled with legatees of Moses and assimilated their science of gematria. He subsequently paused in Babylon and received instruction in astrology from an archimage variously called Hermes II, Zoroaster II, and Dawanay.

Upon the surface of an orb
Centrality is everywhere,
So go forth boldly and absorb
The knowledge every land can spare.

At Delphi, Pythagoras underwent initiation at the hand of the Pythia of the age, Theoclea. She sent him onward to Crete for further purification. The priests of Moros purged him with a meteoric thunderstone. By day he lay face-down beside the ocean; by night he held vigil by a river. Finally, cloaked in black lambskin, he descended into the Idaean cave, and remained there for twenty-seven days.

There is a station none may reach
Except by going underground;
The sage must leave the stream and beach
To be, with darkness, duly crowned.

Pythagoras now went forth to establish his school. As its seat, he chose Croton on the eastern shore of Italy. People flocked to his orations, and a circle of devoted students soon surrounded him.

Pythagoras could hear the mellifluous hum of the universe, the Music of the Spheres. He gave each student a melody pitched to hasten the unfoldment of the student's soul. The ill and infirm were given special songs to heal and restore them.

Melodic strains comprised his cures:
For each, a daily dose of notes.
And thanks to his incessant tours,
These drugs soon buzzed in countless throats.

Everywhere he traveled he taught the ideal of freedom, and before long Italy's petty tyrants began to seriously rethink their ways. For the circle of Pythagoras, harmony and friendship meant everything, and oppression of every kind was anathema.

Like Solomon, Pythagoras knew the languages of animals. He pacified a ravenous bear, persuaded an ox to refrain from eating beans, and hailed an eagle flying overhead, causing it to swoop down and perch on his wrist.

A Siberian skywalker, Abaris, glided to Italy and sought him out. Abaris presented Pythagoras with the golden arrow that had directed his floating steps, since he recognized the Samian sage as a personification of the Hyperborean Apollo, like himself.

The golden arrow led him to
The counterpart he had to meet.
He traveled overland, but flew
So that no cobble touched his feet.

Zalmoxis, a Thracian shaman, was Pythagoras's aide-de-camp, and later spread his teachings along the Danube.

A citizen of Croton named Cylon applied to join Pythagoras's circle, but as his temperament was incurably turbulent, Pythagoras declined to admit him. Seething with resentment, Cylon formed a cabal devoted to the destruction of the Pythagoreans. On a fateful day, Cylon's syndicate set fire to the Pythagoreans' meeting hall, causing the death of the majority of them.

If enemies beleaguer you,
It doesn't signify a fault.
The paragon of friendship too
Endured a terrible assault.

Pythagoras managed to escape, but his heart was broken. The father of Greek philosophy retreated to the Temple of the Muses in Metapontum, abstained from food, and died after forty days.

But no one who dies really dies.

Star Lady

As Pythagoras wandered the White Sea, among the groves beside the Ganges another lion of wisdom wandered. A Scythian prince by birth, he had renounced his perquisites when an excursion beyond the gilded gates of his ancestral villa opened his eyes to the immensity of the world's pain. As you may have guessed, I refer to Gautama, the Buddha Shakyamuni.

The Buddha saw that all beings ache
And ignorance is hardly bliss.
He taught the way to finally wake
Beyond samsara's sad abyss.

Shakyamuni's tale is well known. Less familiar is the story of Tara.

On a faraway planet in a long-ago age lived a princess named Jnanachandra, "Moon of Knowledge." She was known to spend her days in worship and her nights in meditation. A party of monks were sufficiently impressed to offer her a piece of unsolicited advice. They suggested she aspire to attaining a male incarnation, so that the doors of full enlightenment would open to her.

With unruffled sangfroid, Jnanachandra replied that, in a world where form is emptiness and emptiness is form, gratuitous

◀ *The spiteful squadron surrounded Gautama. Suddenly, Tara appeared.*

reifications like "male," "female," and "person" comprise the mental stock-in-trade of only the quaintest of greenhorns and mooncalves. Lacking an adequate rejoinder, the monks hastily excused themselves and shuffled away.

Why should her gender represent
A handicap of any kind?
A lady no less than a gent
May realize the Buddha Mind.

By dint of a constant cultivation of noetic prowess coupled with an unwavering dedication to compassion as the pith of all piths, Tara developed the ability to generate pullulating waves of benevolent scintillas. Like a general at war, she sent her armies of kindness out in orderly phalanxes to counter the depredations of evil figments.

Left, right, left, right, left, right, left, right:
She marched them out into the field,
Each one a golden-hearted knight
Intent on making malice yield.

In this way she vanquished one million, one hundred thousand demons. In recognition of her achievements, the Diwan officially designated her Paladiness.

When Jnanachandra died, as all mortals must, her soul migrated to Malakut. Her manifestation in the World of Images occurred in this way: Surveying the tricosm, the jinnic sage Avalokitesvara was brought to tears by the ubiquity of grief in world after world. His tears became a pool, a pink lotus arose in the pool, and Jnanachandra emerged from the lotus. Her name in Malakut was Tara, "Star Lady."

Her goal in life remained the same,
But now her powers had increased:
Dispelling evil was her aim;
Not on her watch would demons feast.

In the world of matter, Gautama took his seat under a fig tree, resolving not to stand up again until he had seen the farther shore of birth and death. Observing what was impending, the figment Mara perceived an opportunity for mischief. He mustered up a regimen of devilish scintillas and led them on a charge.

A good intention never goes
Unheeded by the wicked crew;
They're more than eager to oppose
Every attempt at breaking through.

The spiteful squadron surrounded the fig tree and commenced hurling torrents of outrageous invective. Gautama redoubled his concentration, and suddenly Tara appeared. She laughed, and the foremost goons fell to their knees. With each successive bout of hilarity another rank of imps collapsed. When her eighth peal rang out, Mara sounded the retreat and the malefactors limped away at best speed.

The consequence of Tara's laugh
Is that bad actors disappear.
They realize they've made a gaffe
With repercussions all too clear.

At dawn, Gautama attained enlightenment. He soon began teaching the Middle Way, and seekers flocked to him in ever burgeoning numbers. Two centuries later, Ashoka, king of

Magadha, embraced the Buddha's path, and the creed quickly spread throughout India. The arahant Mahinda brought the sage's message to Serendib, Padmasambhava carried it to Tibet, and Bodhidharma conveyed it to China.

Star Lady continues to battle fiends in Malakut and in Earth's translucid substratum. Her smile and laughter remain her most redoubtable armaments.

Fragrant Mountain

What events befell concurrently in China? Let's peer into the charming palace at the heart of the kingdom of Fucheng. Alas, the scene is not altogether a happy one.

King Miao Chuang and Queen Pao Te frowned when their first child emerged as a girl. The femaleness of their second child again provoked grimaces. When Miao Shan was born—a third confounded nonboy!—they were livid.

The only consolation the king and queen could conceive was the prospect of prestigious sons-in-law. With this aim in view, they raised their daughters to be covetable brides. The first two princesses adapted themselves to the program, but Miao Shan was of another mind. Hymnody, meditation, and the care of vulnerable animals were her sole preoccupations.

The groom for whom the princess pined
Was no mere mortal human male.
The beau toward whom her heart inclined
Was that which shines behind life's veil.

Miao Shan was willing to compromise, but only this far: if she must marry, her betrothed ought to be a practitioner of the medical arts. Miao Chuang's reply was to send her to a convent to reflect on her obduracy. Miao Shan's ruminations at the nunnery, however, proved to be of a different kind: she wandered beyond the stars in an eidolon of jade.

Miao Shan had mysterious friends. Miao Chuang directed the abbess to occupy his daughter with backbreaking toil. Rabbits, doves, and macaques lent their hands and lightened her load. Miao Chuang sent goons to burn the princess's dormitory. The local elementals dispatched a rain cloud to quell the conflagration.

Miao Chuang was relentless; with a stentorian bellow, he ordered his daughter's execution. The deed was attempted with axes and arrows; each time, a malfunction impeded success. When the executioner presently approached Miao Shan with a garrote, it occurred to her that if he failed again he would suffer demotion, or worse.

The executioner, she felt,
Deserved no blame, for all could see,
The penalty of death he dealt
Was simply Miao Chuang's decree.

Moved by compassion, she seized the cord and extinguished her own breath.

Foul fumes stung Miao Shan's chest. She opened her eyes to a pandemonium of slag, ash, fog, and flame. The denizens of the place were doubled over in torment or prostrate in abjection. Miao Shan sealed her eyelids again.

In her marrow pulsed a teal sap steeped in the emotion of the Deity. She drew a profound breath and the gleaming pith converged in her sternum, assuming the form of a seething nimbus. The billow convulsed, burst, and sent coruscating scud hurtling in all directions.

The sufferers raised their heads. The fires were subsiding, the haze lifting, the sky turning azure-blue. A circuitous breeze made tidy piles of the cinders that had hitherto encrusted the ground. Seedlings promptly sprouted from the newly exposed earth.

The land was scorious and wan
And rang with dismal moans and sighs
Until the coming of Miao Shan,
Who brought green shoots and butterflies.

The administrators of Gehenna were displeased. If Fire and Garden were to become indistinguishable, what would incentivize Earthlings to respect the Law? The local magistrate presented Miao Shan with a fuchsia peach. She obligingly tasted it and fell into a deep sleep.

Miao Shan awoke in her terrene body on Fragrant Mountain, an eminence festooned with twisting pines that oozed a vitalizing balsam. For nine years she remained there, studying to perfection the manner in which the trees silently absorbed afflations from the Universal Soul. At the end of this period, a large delegation from the Diwan descended on the mountain to hail and laurelize her.

The Cloud is always wont to fete
A champion of truth and love.
They crowned her with a coronet
Symbolic of the stars above.

Miao Shan's first disciple was a disabled boy from faraway India named Sudhana. She taught him to lay aside his physical fiber and circumambulate the mountain in pneumatic form.

Her second protege was Lung Nü, granddaughter of the Dragon King who lived at the bottom of the East Sea. These two diligent youths became Miao Shan's lifelong companions.

At the palace, Miao Chuang's body had collapsed under the burden of his unmitigated rage. The doctors were not optimistic. The only remedy that could save him now, they collectively pronounced, was an extract derived from the arms and eyes of someone devoid of the minutest soupcon of anger.

Spies scoured the provinces and in due course brought back the report that a lady of nonpareil serenity had been found on Fragrant Mountain. "Bring me her ichor," the king rasped. Agents of the court presented themselves to Miao Shan and described the king's plight. At once she wrung generous quantities of *élan vital* from her arms and eyes, and bottled the serum in an elegantly enameled phial.

The mind that rests in perfect calm,
Forever luminous and pure,
Supplies the most benefic balm,
The best and choicest natural cure.

Miao Chuang quickly recovered. As he was not entirely insensible to decorum, he resolved to visit Fragrant Mountain with Pao Te and acknowledge the anonymous donor. The sight that greeted the pair left them speechless: there stood Miao Shan herself, her arms hanging limp at her sides, her eyes pale and opaque.

Miao Chuang fell to the ground and confessed his remorse. All would be well, Miao Shan replied, if he would follow the path of the Buddha. New lineaments now unfolded from her frame in the fashion of a butterfly breaking free of its chrysalis.

A thousand eyes of diamond and a thousand arms of gold blazed into view. Miao Shan flew into the sky, trailed by Sudhana and Lung Nü.

Thus did a second phase begin
In Miao Shan's life of dauntless peace.
She would henceforth be called Kuan Yin,
"The One Whose Listening Does Not Cease."

Yunan, Iran, India

Across the vast tracts between the White Sea and the Indus River, Persia's star was ascendant. Destiny favored the Hamite prince Cyrus with unprecedented triumphs. He overthrew the Median Empire, seized Anatolia, subjugated the rulers of the steppe, and conquered Susa and Babylon. Freed at last from Babylonian captivity, the Jews hailed Cyrus as a Messiah.

Thus was forged the Achaemenid Empire.

Cyrus's son Cambyses annexed Egypt, but died an untimely death. A period of disarray followed. When the dust settled, Darius, a Scythian of the royal house of Ariya, wore the Achaemenid crown. Under Darius, the empire reached the zenith of its glory.

Darius II was the penultimate Achaemenid sultan; you've told his tale in your *Book of Kings*. Your sterling couplets tell of Darius II's marriage to Nahid, daughter of the Greek king Filqus; how, on account of her sulfurous breath, Darius II sent her back; and how Alexander was born to Nahid in Macedonia, his Persian paternity kept secret.

His father was Daryush, it's true,
But as he grew up in Yunan,
Filqus ensured that no one knew
Of that which linked him to Iran.

Your splendid epic relates how Darius II remarried and had a second son, Darius III, and how Alexander and the latter, ignorant of their blood tie, met three times on the battlefield, leading in the end to Darius III's death.

You narrate as well how, with his last breath, Darius III entreated Alexander to marry his daughter Roxana, and how Alexander fulfilled his wish. But, my revered friend, you've said little more about the peerless Roxana! Let's repair the omission.

Roxana should obtain her due,
For she was more than just a wife;
When Alexander called, she flew
To Hindustan and saved his life.

The martial arts were the nucleus of the extensive education Darius III provided to his daughter. Roxana skillfully wielded an iron mace few others could lift. A line of down grew above her upper lip, hence she was often taken for a man, especially as she was typically seen in a casque and coat of mail.

But the most extraordinary thing about Roxana was her friendship with an angel. In childhood, the angel was her invisible playmate. As a youth, Roxana confided her secret hopes and fears in her. Now, in adulthood, the angel's watchful eye was a constant shield over her life.

The name of Alexander's mother came close to the angel's name. It was Anahita.

Anahita's presence sang in Roxana's blood when water was near. The help Roxana received from the angel always came in aqueous form. When it rained, Anahita was there without fail, murmuring praises of the Deity.

It's time to strike "bad weather" from
The lexicon we all employ,
For when dark rain clouds duly come
It's a lavation to enjoy.

Soon after their marriage, Alexander installed Roxana on the throne of Iran and set off for India to consult sages and enlarge his empire. It wasn't long, however, before an Indian king, Kaydavar by name, checked Alexander's advance, compelling him to request Roxana to rush to his aid with reinforcements. Roxana obliged him and boldly captured Kaydavar and his daughter.

She had won a key victory, but war raged on as other Indian rulers joined the fray and local wizards deployed dizzying cantrips against the unwelcome Persians and Greeks. Still, at every turn Roxana's prowess and Anahita's protective hand staved off disaster.

And when Roxana neared a pond,
The fish all cast their eyes her way.
With swishing tails they swiftly thronged
To see 'Nahita's protege.

Alexander finally returned westward. His quest for sages had not proven altogether in vain: he brought back with him the Brahmin savant Calanus.

At Istakhr, Alexander and Roxana parted ways, never to meet again.

In your immortal book, you say that Alexander then journeyed to the Land of Darkness and built the wall that kept out Gog and Magog. But those are the deeds of Oghuz Khan.

Shah Alexander traveled far
But never to the land of night,

And after Hindustan his star
No longer burned so red and bright.

Not to worry; many others have made the same mistake. The truth, however, is that Alexander's death in Babylon took place not long after his return from India.

In the centuries that followed, travel, trade, and intellectual exchange between Yunan, Iran, Turan, and India swelled. Statues of the Buddha in Gandhara took on an unmistakably Hellenistic cast, while in Athens, Jataka tales were on everyone's lips.

A corridor was realized
By dint of Alexander's zest;
Thereby two worlds were harmonized:
The Indic East and Grecian West.

The Queen Mother of the West

Alexander, the world conqueror, died at the age of thirty-two.

The preponderance of actors on history's stage appear only for a scene or two. They are born, grow up, make their mark for better or worse, and disappear. Their subsequent exploits and reckonings occur in Malakut, and are visible only to those with eyes of Marij.

There are a few exceptions, of course: beings of supernatural longevity. Among these rare immortals may be counted Melchizedek, Utnapishtim, and Khizr. And let us not forget the elemental hierophant Xiwangmu, the Queen Mother of the West.

To live forever—there's a feat!
But as the mortal tide rolls by,
How piteously bittersweet
To watch so many live and die.

The redoubts of the sages are frequently cavernous hermitages discreetly recessed in glaciated massifs, always far from the beaten track and discoverable only by rarest chance or, more

◀ *Xiwangmu's palace is a portal between the dense and subtle worlds.*

likely, auspicious destiny. Shambhala comes to mind, as does Uttarakuru, the refuge of the siddhas on Mount Meru. Belvodye in the Altai is such a place, as is Muztagh Ata in the Pamirs. In the Kunlun Mountains between Tibet and Xinjiang, Xiwangmu maintains a sanctuary of this kind.

She does not wish to be disturbed,
Except by those rare human souls
With heart aflame and ego curbed,
Pursuing altruistic goals.

Xiwangmu's palace is nestled in a crag of solid jade. The arrangement of its agate pavilions, crystalline pools, porphyry arcades, and copses of peach trees induces an aesthetic rapture so bewildering as to convince visitors that they've died and entered the hereafter.

The limpid rills, the gleaming domes—
It's all enough to make you think
That in these jeweled catacombs
You've overstepped Earth's final brink.

You wouldn't be altogether wrong. The palace is a portal between the dense and subtle worlds. Only fairy peaches grow in the high Kunlun.

The sight of Xiwangmu herself is no less marvelous. Her face and form are those of a prepossessing human woman, but she has a leopard's tail and tiger's teeth. Her robe is of varicolored irisate brocade, a sword hangs at her hip, and on her head a coruscating diadem rests on a mass of disheveled hair. When she ventures out, she rides a chariot of lilac-purple clouds.

The Mandate of Heaven

We spoke of the Yellow Emperor and his teachers, Xuan Nü and Su Nü. The latter were disciples of Xiwangmu. In fact, it was she who referred him to them.

A long line of emperors followed after Huang Di. Every one of them hoped for the blessing of Xiwangmu. Nothing else so clearly confirmed the Mandate of Heaven.

Each Chinese ruler rightly knew
That true dominion comes from God,
And sought, therefore, from Xiwangmu
A sign of Heaven's needful nod.

Xiwangmu bestowed sundry tokens on the wise emperor Shun, including a miraculous tube that enabled him to harmonize the eight winds. Yu, founder of the Xia dynasty, had the privilege of becoming Xiwangmu's direct pupil.

Huang Di, the august patriarch,
And sagely Shun and saintly Yu,
Might all have stumbled in the dark
Had it not been for Xiwangmu.

But as time passed, philosopher kings proved a rare breed. Power corrupts, and it's an unusual soul that can stay humble while enchaired on the Dragon Throne.

Mu was among the mightiest rulers of the long-enduring Zhou dynasty. Wishing to get to know him, Xiwangmu summoned him to her sanctuary. They toasted each other beside her Turquoise Pool and conversed in stanzas of elegant verse.

Moved by an ineffable magnetism, Xiwangmu proposed that Mu stay as her mate and share in her immortality. An incredible honor. But Mu's head was filled with vendettas and dreams of conquest. He bade her a wistful goodbye and descended the mountain.

How restless is the human mind:
Inimical to ease and peace,
Oblivious to truth, and blind
To all that lies beyond caprice!

Later kings likewise flailed about.

Qin Shi Huang bears credit for unifying China and founding the Qin dynasty. His achievements were great but, alas, his missteps were greater. All would have been well had he consulted Xiwangmu.

Qin Shi Huang regarded savants and mystics as nothing but a canker on the body politic. He executed them en masse and made a bonfire of their books. By his decree every school of thought was banned, with the single exception of Legalism.

Condole the stuffy magistrate,
For exoteric learnedness
Can in no measure duplicate
The flutter of an angel's kiss.

Too late, Qin Shi Huang realized that he had destroyed the scrolls that preserved the secret of immortality. And there was nothing he wanted more than to escape death. He had, moreover, snubbed Xiwangmu, closing a crucial avenue.

Seeing only dead ends on the mainland, Qin Shi Huang dispatched the navigator Xu Fu to search the seas for the fabled Mount Penglai, where the elixir of immortality was sure to be found. Following a series of adventures, including a perilous confrontation with a leviathan, Xu Fu discovered Japan.

On Mount Kinryu, a bright-eyed hermit presented Xu Fu with the elixir he had so long sought. But the tonic was intended for him alone, and Xu Fu did not return to China.

No one but you can win your goal;
You must, yourself, set out to seek
The draught that makes the broken whole
And gives the wan a new physique.

Fear of death obsessed Qin Shi Huang, and his carking thoughts turned constantly to the Turks in the north. As a precaution, he mobilized men in droves to elevate and expand Oghuz Khan's ancient wall. In this way the Great Wall of China had its genesis.

A second Oghuz Khan was rising among the tribes of the Xiongnu. His name was Modu Chanyu.

In Modu Chanyu rose a man
Devoted to the holy way.
His call reached far beyond his clan,
Inspiring myriads to pray.

Modu Chanyu sprang from the Göktürks, a bloodline descended from the shamaness Ashina. Ashina was a past master in the Enochian technique of theriomorphism.* The animal form she invariably assumed was that of a gray wolf.

And when the forest heard her howl
A hundred wolves wailed their salute,
And in his tree the wise old owl
Submitted a respectful hoot.

Qin Shi Huang's alteration of Oghuz Khan's wall provoked the ire of the Xiongnu. The confederacy's indignation deepened when the emperor seized a portion of their territory, the Ordos plateau. The result was centuries of skirmishes punctuated by spasms of all-out war.

Foreboding whelmed Qin Shi Huang. The thought of Azrael made his pulses race. He commissioned six thousand terracotta warriors to guard his tomb. A meteor fell, a bad portent. The potions he drank to extend his life sickened him, and he closed his eyes for the last time.

The hour of death at last had come,
And one by one his senses failed.
His nervous system too went numb,
And off into the blue he sailed.

Xiwangmu sighed. Since the time of the Three Sovereigns and Five Emperors long, long ago, the emperors of China had so rarely attained Heaven's Mandate. But there was a consolation. There were other potentates: the sages of the Tao.

What need for consecrated monarchs when the likes of Lao Tzu walked the Earth? Lao Tzu, that inimitable Scythian drifter with a heart outstripping time and space and not a care in the world—to whom else could Xiwangmu have dictated her *Tao Te Ching*?

The author of the Tao Te Ching
Was she who wears the Western crown,
And wise Lao Tzu, that realmless king,
Is he to whom she passed it down.

And then there was the admirable Chuang Tzu.

One day Chuang Tzu was fishing in a pond. A pair of dignitaries approached with the news that the king wished to honor him with the coveted post of chief minister. With gaze fixed on the water, Chuang Tzu made reference to a mummified turtle that the king kept in a chest on his altar. He queried the officials, "Would the turtle prefer to retain its sanctity in the reliquary or wriggle in the mud?" The pair answered that the turtle would doubtlessly rather live and breathe. To this Chuang Tzu replied, "Begone then, and let me wriggle in the mud!"

Xiwangmu smiled when the incident was reported to her. *There* is an emperor, she thought.

Yes, there among the frogs and cranes
Sat one who knew the ways of God.
Let others have ambitious brains,
Chuang Tzu enjoyed his reel and rod.

Burning Water

In China, devotees of the Queen Mother of the West largely succeeded in keeping in check the abominable practice of human sacrifice. Across the Ocean of Kiwa, however, that appalling enormity became commonplace. Figments had deluded the priests of the Nahua into believing, as a matter of unshakable religious conviction, that the sun required for its nourishment throbbing hearts exhumed from the chests of men, women, and children.

Mortified, Hurakhsh sent up an appeal to the Deity. An injunction reached the Diwan, and the ministers set to work. They found the soul they needed in the limbo of Venus. Ce Acatl he was called. On Earth he would be named Quetzalcoatl, "Plumed Serpent."

His name foretells what he'd explain,
The meditative yogic rite
By which the tailbone and the brain—
Or snake and bird—at last unite.

His human parents were Chimalma and Mixcoatl. When Chimalma conceived, with inner eyes she saw the Emerald Rock. They say, therefore, that she "swallowed an emerald" to bring Quetzalcoatl into the world.

◀ *The tailbone and the brain—or snake and bird—at last unite.*

Like his father, Quetzalcoatl distinguished himself as a warrior. But he did much more. He profitably mined precious lodes, brought the virtues of cacao and cotton to his people's attention, and innovated new methods of pottery and weaving.

These breakthroughs did not come to him by trial and error. Quetzalcoatl's knowledge was revealed.

Down here below all that is known
Has come from sources you know not.
You think you find, but you are shown;
Don't claim invention—you were taught.

Quilaztli, a priestess in the line of Votan, was his instructor. But her teachings merely restored to him the memory of what he had been taught before birth in the Basilica of the Diwan.

He had learned in the Basilica to call upon the One and commune with the Soul of Souls. And this he now did. At midnight he would kneel on the mossy bank of a spring. Fasting had essentialized his flesh. Arrayed in quetzal plumes, he pierced his skin with turquoise thorns along meridians that had been shown to him. His diaphane, eidolon, and nous* stirred to alertness. From the material of his mind he fashioned shimmering scintillas in the shapes of snakes, birds, and butterflies, all lofted high into the spheres on a current of prayerful attention.

He would find himself in a station he called the Place of Duality. Multiplicity was annihilated; his soul was alone with the One. Then his soul forgot itself, and knowledge came. The seeds of the future were given into his hands.

The station of Duality
Lies at the edge of Unity,
Between the One Reality
And Life's profuse community.

The people saw that he was like no one else. They urged him to establish a city and be their king and highpriest. He obliged them and laid out the plan of Tollan. The city was a replica of the universe. Quetzalcoatl's people, the Toltecs, devoted themselves to the arts, and flourished beyond anyone's dreams.

As highpriest of Tollan, Quetzalcoatl sternly outlawed human sacrifice. He explained that gore was superfluous and moreover anathema to Heaven. What was needed was to marry fire and water and in this way make the solar heart blossom.

Allow the snake to be a bird
And let pure water burn and glow.
Forget all that you erstwhile heard;
Your heart knows all you need to know.

Infuriated by the proscription of their cult, the priests of the figments commenced plotting.

Quetzalcoatl's face was a ruin of pockmarks. While his pursuivants saw only his perfection, his enemies mocked his disfigurement. The sorcerer Tezcatlipoca brought a mirror and fleered sinisterly as he held it up to the king's face. Quetzalcoatl was taken aback, but declined to abdicate. Instead he commissioned a turquoise mask wreathed in spoonbill plumes, which he wore from that day onward.

The face each human being wears
Is but a sculpted mask, no more,

And when souls fly back to their lairs
They let their masks fall to the floor.

The sorcerers now tried another tack. They brewed a heady pulque of maguey and insisted he drink. Quetzalcoatl first refused, then allowed himself a taste, and finally gulped great cupfuls. The intoxication that followed left him depleted and ashamed.

Quetzalcoatl undertook a rigorous penance and restored himself. But the incident convinced him that his kairos had reached its conclusion. He sang songs of endings and an abysmal dolor drenched the city.

For four days Quetzalcoatl lay in a funeral urn. Then he rose up, buried his artifacts beneath the moss beside his spring, and left Tollan.

Beneath the moss are hidden things,
But seizing them would be a crime.
Only a serpent bearing wings
May have them, come the proper time.

He traveled first to the Black Land, then to the Red Land, and finally to the Land of Fire. The third tract takes its name from the actions Quetzalcoatl performed there. His companions watched in bewilderment.

He stood in his mask and plumes. A tear fell from his eye. When the drop struck the ground, a great flame jagged up and engulfed his body. The flame produced neither smoke nor heat. Quetzalcoatl's form became swirling ash, the ash becoming birds of many colors: pink spoonbills, turquoise cotingas, scarlet-and-green trogons, periwinkle herons, particolored parrots. Then, in the flash of an instant, the murmuration coalesced into a single bird, an emerald quetzal.

The quetzal soared high and disappeared in the empyrean.

When four days passed, up in the sky
Old Venus flashed and roiled the gloam,
And there were tears in every eye,
For Quetzalcoatl had gone home.

The Son of Man

When the Achaeans under Agamemnon sacked Troy, the Turanian prince Aeneas was among the small number of Trojans to survive. With a band of companions, Aeneas abandoned Anatolia in search of a new beginning. The Aeneads eventually made their way to the Italian peninsula, where they laid the seeds of Rome.

Homer, Orpheus's heir, predicted that Aeneas's descendants would rule the Trojans. In Italy or Anatolia? Both, these descendants hoped. Nor did they merely hope. Emboldened by Alexander's audacious example, they took Sicily, Iberia, Macedonia, and Carthage. Anatolia, Syria, Judea, Gaul, and Egypt followed in due course, and later, Albion and Arabia.

The Pax Romana thus cohered,
A golden age, so some would say,
And it was then that he appeared:
The sign of God's life, truth, and way.

Under Cyrus's auspices the Jews, newly liberated from Babylon, rebuilt Solomon's Temple on a modest scale. When Rome assumed control of Judea, the empire's vassal Herod considerably expanded this Second Temple, restoring its former architectural splendor.

During these renovations, which lasted almost a century, a pious young lady named Mary served for a time in the Temple staff. Her life, however, was soon to be indelibly altered.

Maryam: that was the name of she
Who swept the Temple's limestone floor
In such exalted ecstasy
Her broom became the stuff of lore.

As Mary sat at ease one day, watching the play of light on an adobe wall, the glitter strangely intensified, becoming almost unbearably bright. She blinked, and a dazzling figure stood before her, anthropic in form but composed solely of radiance: Gabriel.

In sibilant tones, the archangel asked whether she was willing to be the mother of a holy child. Without pausing to weigh the matter, Mary signaled her assent. A cloak of hers was lying nearby. Gabriel picked it up, breathed into it. This done, Gabriel bowed and disappeared.

Mary wrapped herself in the cloak, and a new sensation filled her. Not long after, she discovered she was carrying a child.

The father of the holy child
Was nothing other than Pure Breath.
They say, on being born he smiled,
And for him there would be no death.

The sight of a propitious comet led three Magian astrologers to expect Jesus's birth. They traveled to Jerusalem to inquire with Herod as to the possible existence in his kingdom of an extraordinary child. The tyrant grew alarmed and issued orders that newborn boys should not be allowed to live until the danger had passed. Learning of the decree, Mary fled to Egypt and raised her son among the palms of the Nile.

Jesus's cousin John was a prophet and the son of a prophet. When Jesus reached the age of thirty, John baptized him in the waters of the Jordan River and directed him to the wilderness. For forty days, Jesus fasted and prayed. Three times Iblis attempted to lure him off course, failing at each turn. Day by day, the aureole encircling Jesus's head grew brighter.

Out there beneath the starry sky
The son of Mary basked in peace,
A sapphire ease as deep and high
As boundless space, without surcease.

Even after departing the desert, Jesus's way of life was of utmost simplicity. Beyond the patched woolen robe he wore, he owned next to nothing. Stones were his pillows.

His work was to make the outer like the inner. To this end, he made his way to Galilee. The fishermen were drawn to him. He reeled them in the way they reeled in fish. But his closest disciples were three women, all named Mary: his mother, his sister, and Mary Magdalene.

Jesus said he was not a teacher. He was the guardian of a bubbling spring. Those who drank from it would lose themselves and find the Deity.

One day as he walked with his disciples, on the side of the road the rotting corpse of a dog came into view. The disciples winced and turned away. But Jesus approached the carcass with nonchalance, and said, "What lovely white teeth it has."

The others only saw the lees,
But Jesus saw the crystal wine,

For eyes of light see as they please
And, seeing beauty, brightly shine.

At an Asclepion in Jerusalem the infirm sat beside a pool waiting for the genius loci to stir the waters and heal them. One of the patients lay paralyzed. Jesus came and instructed him to get up. To the astonishment of everyone, he did just that.

This was but one of the many healings Jesus performed. By the vitality of his breath, with the leave of the Deity, he cured the sick, restored sight to the blind, and raised the dead. Hence he was called the Messiah.

There never was a better cure
Than Messianic healing breath,
For nothing else, you may be sure,
Can pry away the grip of death.

In the end, Jesus underwent sublimation and rose through the planes.

In a turbulent vortex in Earth's rolling etherscape he found the jinn archpriestess Pistis Sophia, lost and trapped. He guided her back to her native land in Malakut and unveiled the syzygy in which she stood paired with him. Pistis Sophia's eidolon recovered its ancient glow and she lifted up a song to the Light of Lights.

Sophia's long-lost light returned;
She spread her phosphorescent wings.
For too long in that gyre she'd turned;
She'd bathe now in celestial springs.

Touring Malakut, Jesus exorcized figments, dispersed flocks of noxious scintillas, and set in motion new jet streams for the circulation of light and life. Melchizedek rallied to his call, and the entire Diwan effervesced in activity, like a hive of bees waking from somnolence with the coming of spring.

Jesus now took on etheric contours, returned to his terrestrial disciples, and instructed them in the way of life and work proper to the inner worlds. Celestial fire sprang from their tongues; they spoke strange and marvelous words. And they set out, each in a different direction, to spread the message of the Deity.

The Three Marys

After the sublimation of Jesus, his mother, Mary, lived in a house by the Mount of Zion. Day by day her desire to be reunited with her son grew. When twelve years of anticipation ran their course, a Heavenly herald appeared with the news that the time had come.

Do not resent mortality
Or denigrate sweet Azrael,
For dying's actuality
Is nothing but a parted veil.

The smoke of frankincense whirled in the candlelight. Faces took shape one after the other: Peter, Andrew, James son of Zebedee, John, Philip, Bartholomew, Thomas, Matthew, James son of Alphaeus, Thaddeus, Simon, Judas, Mary Magdalene. The ceiling of Mary's bedroom opened and the stars shone down. In a column of glory, Jesus descended, accompanied by a retinue of celestial ministers.

As lily-white doves enacted an aerial dance of rapturous finesse, a seraphic choir filled the air with song. Then all at once the doves alighted, the music ceased, and Jesus spoke. "Come, my chosen one, come and take my seat. I have missed your beauty."

"My heart is ready," Mary answered. At once, a blazing cloud

engulfed mother and son and bore them to the highest reaches of Heaven.

She lived henceforth in Illiyin,
Afloat in tides of mystic grace,
A perfect saint and holy queen,
Enrobed in luminescent lace.

Mary Magdalene had been a lady of wealth and a bon vivant. When she met Jesus, her life took an entirely new course. Tears came often to her eyes. She washed the Messiah's feet and placed herself at his service. Jesus treated her with immense tenderness. She became his closest disciple.

After Jesus left the world, villains rounded up as many of his disciples as they could find, threw them in a dilapidated rudderless hull, and sent it adrift on the White Sea. Among those consigned to death in this fashion was Mary Magdalene. But the boat did not capsize. Benevolent elementals buoyed it with care and speedily propelled it to the port of Marseilles in the south of Gaul.

When lost at sea, do not despair,
For you are never quite alone.
Lift up an earnest heartfelt prayer,
Then look and see where you are blown.

The citizens of Marseilles were suspicious of the foreigners and did not readily open their doors to them. Mary Magdalene found shelter in the portico of a temple haunted by a nebulous figment.

One day the prince of the province and his wife visited the

◀ *For dying's actuality is nothing but a parted veil.*

temple to offer prayers in the hope of conceiving a child. Mary Magdalene advised the couple to pray directly to the Deity. They gave her little notice, but Mary was not to be brushed off so easily; she visited them in their dreams and repeated her admonition.

Finding Mary impossible to ignore, the couple sought her out in the temple portico and listened to all she had to say. There was no doubt as to the immaculacy of the breath blowing in her words, and they found themselves moved to offer lodgings to the Christian exiles. With Mary's blessing, the prince's wife soon conceived.

The couple had a change of heart
By cause of Mary's truthful speech;
Their reservations fell apart
And wisdom flew into the breach.

Even still, they were not fully prepared to adopt the faith of Jesus; they insisted on consulting the apostle Peter. What was the need, when the apostle of apostles stood before them? Nonetheless, Mary Magdalene indulged their fancy and explained that Peter could be found in Rome.

The couple set sail at once. Along the way a storm shook the ship, causing the prince's wife to deliver her child prematurely, and in doing so, to die. Since the child could not be expected to survive without mother's milk, the sailors insisted that the deceased lady and her ill-fated child be left on a nearby islet. Seeing no alternative, the prince acquiesced.

How truly tragic was the scene;
His cherished wife and child were gone,
And though affliction gripped his spleen,
There was no choice but to press on.

In Rome, Peter consoled the widower and promised all would be well. Tentatively encouraged, the prince followed Peter to Jerusalem and paid his respects at the places sacred to Jesus's memory. Two years passed in this way, after which the prince took passage on a vessel returning to Marseilles. When the ship neared the rock where he had left behind his wife and child, he persuaded the captain to allow him to briefly debark.

To his endless astonishment, the prince found a toddler throwing stones into the sea. His son! The boy led him to his mother, who lay under the cloak the prince had draped over her. The prince knelt next to the prostrate form and beseeched Mary Magdalene's help. His wife arose, alive. She had been with Mary Magdalene these past two years, ethereally visiting the holy places of Jerusalem alongside Peter and the prince.

The family returned to Gaul, swore their devotion to the way of Jesus, and spread the message of the Deity far and wide. Her worldly mission now complete, Mary Magdalene retreated to a cave in the wilderness and gave herself over to perpetual meditation. The few fortunate souls who caught a glimpse of her in those years observed that when she prayed, she floated in the air.

Her feet were marvels in themselves;
No one had witnessed such a pair,
For like the feet of faes and elves,
They trod on ground, but also air.

Regarding Jesus's sister Mary, almost nothing is known. She must be counted among the holy ones whose lives are entirely veiled. It is enough that the Deity knows their secrets. In the end, only the One is the knower.

Balinus

Rome's persecution of the followers of Jesus was not slow to begin. Nero initiated the carnage, and it continued in waves for three centuries. In Ephesus, the Seven Sleepers saved themselves by sheltering in a cave. This to the side, many of the faithful were martyred.

The faith that meets cruel nails with calm
And doesn't flinch before a fire
Holds Heaven's grace within its palm
And stands unburnt above a pyre.

The Roman Jew Paul initially persecuted the Christians but then, in a remarkable turn of events, became their most vocal champion. Reports of Jesus's teaching varied. Indited by unknown compilers, the gospels of Matthew, Mark, Luke, and John rose to the forefront. But other accounts also circulated, including gospels ascribed to Thomas, Philip, and Mary Magdalene. Jesus's nature and mission was a subject of running debates. The momentousness of his coming was apparent, but what did it mean?

Something was in the air; it wasn't only the Christians that felt it. Jesus's deeds in Malakut had ushered in a new era. Baleful figments were on the back foot and a new dispensation was pouring into the world.

The world was witnessing a dawn,
A flowering of nascent light.
The World Soul seemed as though a swan
With outsplayed wings prepared for flight.

Apollonius of Tyana never met Jesus, but that did not prevent him from reflecting the Christ spirit. Like Pythagoras before him, he traveled the world weaving threads of wisdom. An Anatolian by birth, he consorted with magi in Babylon, yogis in India, gymnosophists in Ethiopia, and assorted mystagogues in Egypt and Yunan. Under the pyramid of Hermes, he inspected the Emerald Tablet. He would be the last to do so, and it is because of him that the inscription is known to the world.

When an officer at the gates of Babylon asked Apollonius how he imagined he could enter without proper papers, he answered, "The whole Earth is mine."

And what was Apollonius's was for everyone.

Once, on the outskirts of Ephesus, he was discoursing on the importance of sharing the good things of life. A little flock of sparrows sat listening silently in a nearby tree. Just then, another sparrow arrived, twittered animatedly, and led the sparrows away. Apollonius explained that the sparrows in the tree had been invited to a feast: a short distance away, a boy had dropped some kernels of corn, and the sparrow who discovered the windfall wished to share it. Seized by curiosity, Apollonius's audience sprinted down the road to discover that matters were exactly as he had described.

The way of Apollonius
Boils down to love and confrerie.
For him, to be harmonious
Conveys the essence of esprit.

Alexandria

A new wind had blown into Judea. Some Jews became Christians, others Gnostics. And then there were the Zealots, who read the signs of the times as a call to arms against Roman hegemony. The result was tragedy. In the course of three wars Herod's Temple was leveled, multitudes of Jews and Romans perished, and the Jews were driven from Jerusalem and dispersed to the ends of the Earth.

Hadrian consigned the eminent Rabbi Akiva to prison. To escape persecution, his pupil Shimon bar Yochai retreated to a cave in Palestine. For years he intoned the Name of the Deity. When he ultimately emerged, he carried an enormous stack of inscribed sheets. The title of the book was *Zohar.*

The Book of Splendor thus appeared,
The ur-text of all Kabbalah,
Of all midrashim most revered*
*By Talmudists, subhanallah.**

The cultures of Judea and Rome were not always at odds. The illustrious Philo, a contemporary of Jesus and Apollonius, read the Bible in the light of Plato, and vice versa. Philo was a resident of Alexandria, that great lighthouse of a city.

Alexander never lived to see the excellence he had created

The sunset of the Egyptian mysteries was breathtaking.

in laying the foundations of Alexandria in the Nile delta. It was there that the third Hermes would compose the seventeen books of the *Corpus Hermeticum*. Hermes III worked quietly; nothing is known of the circumstances of his life.

Or *her* life. Could Hermes III have been Maria the Jewess, who famously said, "One becomes two, two becomes three, and out of the third comes the one as the fourth?" Or Cleopatra the Alchemist, author of the *Chrysopoeia*?

The sunset of the Egyptian mysteries was breathtaking. The priest Zosimus and his soror mystica, Theosebia, synthesized the temple arts of the Egyptian House of Life with Solomonic metallurgy and Gnostic theology to express an alchemical philosophy of penetrating insight and universal appeal.

The puffers were preoccupied
With trying to manufacture gold,

While alchemists that delved inside
Themselves discovered troves untold.

Alexandria's deepest thinkers were the quietest. Next to nothing is known of Ammonius Saccas. As the teacher of the pagan Plotinus and the Christian Origen, however, his influence was immense. In the wake of Plato and Aristotle, Greek philosophy had drifted into shallow waters. Plotinus and his heirs—Porphyry, Iamblichus, and Proclus—recovered something of the old shamanic sap, albeit wrapped up in dusty syllogisms.

Rome took a dizzying turn when Constantine embraced the faith of Christ. Christians everywhere celebrated, but in truth it was a mixed blessing. Worldly success proves all too often a spiritual detriment. In a matter of years Christians went from the persecuted to persecutors.

They say that when a potentate
Installs a dervish at his side,
The king obtains a blessed fate;
Not so the dervish—woe betide!

Constantine ordered the closure of the Serapeum of Alexandria, where the Ptolemies had preserved the lore of Kemet. Alexandrians roused themselves, but Roman forces overwhelmed them and razed the complex to the ground. Throughout the empire, libraries were burning.

Nor were books the only victims. Hypatia was the brilliant doyenne of the leading Platonic school of Alexandria. A mob of boors calling themselves followers of Christ attacked her in the street, tore her apart, and burned her remains.

The spirit of Alexandria died that day.

They'd carried out a turpitude;
Above, a million angels wept,
While down below, the city's mood
Was desolate, and no one slept.

There were, however, true lovers of Sophia among the devotees of Jesus. In Edessa and Jerusalem, Stephen bar Sudayli transmitted profound traditions of meditation and ecstasy traced to the Holy Hierotheus, an enigmatic disciple of Paul. This lineage found full flower in the theology of Dionysius the Areopagite, an adept as elusive as Hierotheus himself.

Dionysius posited beauty as the source of all things. His writings are works of unexampled loveliness.

While some were burning books and shrines,
The friends of God were occupied
With Allah's beatific signs,
Afloat on Heaven's glistening tide.

Blood and Snow

Before Jesus ascended through the spheres he called his disciples to a modest banquet in Jerusalem. As they arrived, in spite of their humble protestations, he washed their feet. Before him on the table stood Melchizedek's emerald cup.

Melchizedek had proffered to
The Patriarch a loaf and draught;
This practice Christ restored anew,
To juvenate the priestly craft.

Jesus was not seen again in the flesh. In spirit, however, he appeared to Joseph of Arimathea, a man of fine fiber. Jesus gave the Grail into his care, instructing him to entrust it to his brother-in-law Brons. Brons was to convey the relic to Albion and guard it there as Grail Keeper of the age.

Jesus's deeds in Malakut left the figments in frantic disarray. They convened a hasty conference to evaluate their options. The consensus was that they needed an antichrist.

The figments hatched an evil plan:
They'd labor to bring forth a child
Who'd grow into a wicked man
And cause the world to be defiled.

They found an elemental of surly disposition; this would be the father. As mother, they chose the daughter of an old Gaulish family fallen on hard times. In Malakut, they intercepted a guileless soul on the verge of incarnation and planted sorcerous seeds in his mind. As he grew up, they would rear those seeds and lead him down the path of evil.

A perfect plan, or so it seemed. The abomination was committed as the young lady slept. But the plan was not perfect. The young mother's stainless conscience attracted a ray from the Deity. The dart immunized the child from the susurrations of devils. The figments' intended proxy would be, instead, the Diwan's agent.

A hybrid is what Merlin was;
A child of sorcery, it's true,
But also Heaven's son because
His mother was an ingénue.

When Merlin was born his mother was put on trial for fornication, a capital offense. The boy could already speak, and didn't hesitate to leap to his mother's defense. He pointed out that she had no active involvement in his conception, and moreover, the judge's family had a colorful history of its own. The case was closed.

If you would play the haughty judge,
My friend, take care whom you accuse;
Are you prepared to duly trudge
A mile in her painful shoes?

Merlin's powers waxed year by year, and word spread of his uncanniness. And so it was that Vortigern summoned him on a blustery day.

Vortigern had usurped Albion's throne from the house of Constantine. He first made Constantine's successor, Constans, his puppet; then, when an assassin took the prince's life—presumably on Vortigern's order—he hastily claimed the throne himself. Constans's younger brothers, Aurelius and Uther, retreated to Breton and bided their time.

It now fell to Vortigern to stave off the Picts and Scots that had harried his predecessors. In doing so, he made the fatal error of reinforcing his army with Saxon mercenaries. Seeing that Vortigern stood on weak knees and Albion's fields were loamy, the Saxons ushered in an invasion from the continent. Vortigern fled to Wales and attempted the construction of an impenetrable castle.

All things are prone to dissipate
And everyone is left bereft,
But most of all, a dire fate
Befalls the hand enriched by theft.

The castle refused to be built. Time and again, walls collapsed as soon as they were raised. Vortigern's astrologers solemnly pronounced that only the blood of a half-man would dispel the curse. Merlin was accordingly summoned.

Chiding the astrologers for their dilettantism, Merlin explained the actual problem: two dragons, of mutually hostile attitude, slept under the foundation. The bedrock was excavated and there indeed sprawled a pair of scaled hulks.

A pair of worms couched underground,
One crimson and the other white.
For long they'd waited there, rockbound,
Now freed, their instinct was to fight.

Springing from quiescence, they violently contended until the red dragon lay dead, whereupon the white dragon winged away.

Merlin had bad news for Vortigern. The vanquished red dragon, he said, represented Vortigern himself. Its vanquisher signified the princes now arriving on Albion's shore, Aurelius and Uther.

Merlin withheld the deeper meaning of the event. Red bespeaks the appetites of the human heart; white, the angelic life of the soul. Vortigern personified the roughest of mortal motivations. But the sons of Constantine were only a prelude to the coming of a full-fledged angel-man. In him, the white dragon would find its perfect expression.

The angel-man would in turn prepare the way for the complete epiphany of smaragdine green, the advent of the Seal of the Prophets. But time was needed for this, and Merlin would have an important part to play in all of it.

The ivory worm's ascendancy
Was by no means a sudden fact,
For long endures the tendency
Of opposites to interact.

The brothers duly arrived, overthrew the usurper, and pushed back the Saxons. The Saxons had toppled numerous churches; Aurelius promptly rebuilt them. To memorialize Albion's fallen defenders, he directed Merlin to import from Erin a circle of eldritch megaliths anciently brought over from Africa by Fomors. "Stonehenge" the ring has come to be called.

Little time passed before a vengeful son of Vortigern conspired with the Saxons to stage an insurrection. Still more villainously, he contrived to have Aurelius poisoned. As Aurelius lay dying in London, in the night sky a gossamer dragon shot out of a blinking star. Uther assumed the throne with a heavy heart and swiftly routed the Saxons. Merlin, his chief minister, dubbed him "Uther Pendragon."

There was a considerable quantity of vermillion in Uther. He found himself hopelessly infatuated with Igraine, the wife of Gorlois, Duke of Cornwall. When Gorlois rebuked him and sealed away Igraine in the castle Tintagel, Uther waged war. As Gorlois bled out his life on the snowy battlefield, Uther, disguised as the duke by Merlin's magic, entered Tintagel and consummated his passion for Igraine. Arthur was conceived in this way.

Merlin foresaw a grand destiny.

He knew he must not fail to act;
He had to guide King Arthur's days,
And nothing but the Artifact
Would banish the prevailing haze.

A Grand Deception

In view of the irregular circumstances of Arthur's birth, Merlin thought it best that the child be raised in anonymity. Uther died soon after, compelling Merlin to serve as regent. Needless to say, Merlin was not one to covet the crown, and as soon as Arthur reached his fifteenth year the good wizard proclaimed him Uther's heir.

On every face surprise transpired
And wonderment gripped everyone,
For no one knew the king had sired
A living, breathing royal son.

Arthur's first years on the throne were spent subduing popinjays who disputed his authority. Year by year, he proved his mettle and won acclaim. All the while, Albion's prosperity burgeoned apace.

As his seat, Arthur constructed a splendid pile, which he whimsically christened with the Arabic name Kamaalaat, "Manse of Perfections." At the center of the grand hall stood his father's Round Table. It was at this board that he convened his flower of chivalry.

The table's famed rotundity
Was no mere accident of chance;

It tokened a profundity:
The stars trace circles as they dance.

All of the knights of the Round Table were bannerets of the first order, but one stood out as a paladin without equal. This was Lancelot du Lac. The orphaned son of a Gaulish king and queen, Lancelot grew up in the care of the orionid sibyl Nimué, better known as the "Maiden of the Lake." Even now, her aegis continued to expedite his affairs in all respects.

Excalibur—you've heard the name?
It came to Arthur as a boon
From Nimué of ancient fame
Beneath a visionary moon.

Thirteen chairs were ranged around the Round Table. Twelve were populated, but the thirteenth stood vacant. The "Siege Perilous" it was called, and only the hero favored to attain the Grail would survive the attempt to occupy it. The identity of the anticipated champion remained unknown.

The Grail glowed in the tenuitous castle Corbenic, guarded by the Fisher King Pelles and his daughter Helizabel. The day of its revelation had not yet come, but everyone felt in their bones that with Arthur on the throne, the awaited divulgence could not be far off.

With bated breath, they hoped and prayed
The Grail would consecrate the land.
They longed to see the world remade
By way of Heaven's guiding hand.

Could Lancelot be the Grail winner? His qualifications were numerous, and this brought him to the notice of Orc, a malicious figment who had, for years, applied his energies to ensuring that the Grail remained in the background of history rather than the forefront. Anatomizing Lancelot's psyche, the miscreant discovered a primordial affinity between the Chevalier du Lac and Helizabel. Helizabel's face was the image to which the hero's heart was keyed.

The scheming figment saw his chance
To lead Sir Lancelot astray
By means of an askew romance
Resulting in grim disarray.

Certain inhabitants of Malakut boast expertise in phantasmic transposition, an illusionary art by which one image is made to appear in the place of another. Orc was an old hand at the method and employed it now with impressive precision. In Lancelot's occipital lobe, he superimposed Helizabel's face on that of Arthur's queen, Guinevere, and vice versa.

Lancelot found himself in an agonizing position. Arthur was his liege and loyal friend. But the tantalizing allure of Guinevere, whom he took to be Helizabel, drove him to the edge of his wits. To restrain himself from dishonorable conduct he fled Kamaalaat and wandered forest and field alone and distrait.

It was a cruel and hateful prank,
A vile and obnoxious hex.
His heart was good, and rightly shrank
From playing false his sovereign rex.

In Malakut a noble eidolon peered down over the hills and swales of the terrestrial world. The Diwan had prepared this Earth-goer to be born as Galahad and to rise to win the Grail.

Galahad's mother could only be Helizabel, the Grail Bearer. His father could be none other than the one Heaven meant for her, the Chevalier du Lac.

In the way that Arthur kept Merlin by his side, Pelles patronized the wizardess Brisen. Perceiving the mischief that Orc had created, Pelles instructed Brisen to unveil Helizabel's true lineaments to Lancelot's gaze.

Brisen's cure succeeded; Helizabel received Lancelot at the castle of Case, and he saw her as she was. They spent the night in rapture, and Galahad descended to Earth.

Thus was conceived the destined one,
The angelos who'd pierce the veil,
And as Helizabel's own son,
Fulfill the promise of the Grail.

Attainment

It was the Feast of Pentecost and Arthur's knights were assembled around him. Suddenly a woman of courtly bearing burst into the hall, announced herself as a servant of Corbenic, and urged Lancelot to come and perform an accolade straight away. The Chevalier du Lac obligingly followed the earnest messenger to a glade where Galahad, now a young man, stood surrounded by venerable hermitesses and cowled orionids.

He knew not who this squire might be,
But saw him wrapt in fragrant light,
And in his chest surged fresh esprit;
Here was, he knew, a flawless knight.

Lancelot conveyed Galahad to Kamaalaat, and the young man instinctively seated himself in the Siege Perilous. The assembly held its breath. Galahad survived—the seat was rightfully his. As a further confirmation, Galahad casually pulled a sword from a stone beside the river as Merlin nodded knowingly.

The knights all took their seats around the Round Table and pressed Galahad to address them. Helizabel's son spoke in modest but confident tones. He said that nothing could be more important for Albion or the world than the influence of the Grail, the instrument by which the presence of the Deity most

tangibly made itself felt. He urged Arthur to send his chivalry out in search of the holy chalice. With gleaming eyes Arthur gave the requisite order, and the knights rode out.

The tests and trials awaiting the Grail seekers were numerous and varied. Feroce lions, gaping abysses, and intoxicating sirens seemed to loom at every turn. Orc was evidently far from idle.

Before long, the preponderance of the errant knights fell maimed or dead. Numerous others gave up the quest in dejection.

A sacred quest is no small feat;
Grave hardship comes with taking part.
To brave the hoarfrost, mud, and sleet
Requires a courageous heart.

Galahad wandered alone. In the deep forest he came upon a well, the water of which seethed with an unaccountable heat. Galahad dipped his hand in the convulsion. At once it calmed, cooled, and showed him his reflection in lucid lines.

Beyond the forest, in the land of Gorre, rose the cobbled walls of an abbey sheltering a pair of timeworn tombs. The first was imbued with an ambiance of sanctity. This was the resting place of Joseph of Arimathea's son. The second, occupying the crypt, smoldered with lurid spectral flames exuding a fetid miasma. This was the grave of Simeon, a disloyal and belligerent follower of Joseph.

The monks welcomed Galahad and readily assented to his request to visit the crypt. As Galahad invoked the Name of the Deity, the caustic flames subsided, the air cleared, and an incorporeal voice spoke. Simeon's eidolon hailed Galahad and

◀ *The Grail slowly ascended, with Galahad floating after it.*

expressed the fervid conviction that the knight's arrival heralded the Deity's mercy. Galahad exhumed Simeon's remains and reburied them in the churchyard to the unanimous approval of the monks.

The presence of Sir Galahad
Epitomized the grace of God;
His aura made the cheerless glad
And lilies decked the path he trod.

As Galahad rode on, following obscure signs, Percival and then Bors—fellow knights of the Round Table both—crossed his path and made themselves his companions. Soon Corbenic rose ahead, and the three knights entered.

Pelles received them with tears of joy. His son Eleazer, Galahad's uncle, brought out a sword which in bygone times had shattered when an enemy of Joseph of Arimathea had driven it into his thigh. Percival attempted to reattach the pieces, without success. Bors similarly failed, but Galahad succeeded.

The sword was whole again—and now, what was this? Pelles stood with unwonted erectness. A troublesome welt on his own thigh, which had for decades proved unresponsive to treatment, had now suddenly healed.

Thus stood repaired the Fisher King,
Made new thanks to his own grandchild;
Bleak winter's frost was thawed by spring;
He threw aside his cane and smiled.

The doors of the hall swung open. In swept a majestic personage surrounded by an entourage of glowing seraphs. An angelic herald announced, "Joseph of Arimathea stands before you!" Pelles, Eleazer, Percival, Bors, and Galahad performed devout genuflections.

The seraphs erected a table and installed on it an object covered in samite. Joseph invoked the Name of the Deity and held up a loaf of bread and brimming cup. The shimmering silhouettes of Melchizedek, Abraham, Sarah, Hagar, Mary, and Jesus irradiated the hall. A sublime perfume wafted on the breeze as the loaf and cup melted into the air.

The fragrance was the blissful scent
That Seth perceived the day when he
Stood at the Garden Gate and bent
A reverential, grateful knee.

The seraphs now uncovered the emerald chalice. The radiance of a million suns tore away the veils of space and time, and each witness to the moment was whelmed by an inrushing of immensity almost beyond his capacity to bear. Then the Sakina spoke and said, *The Deity is the light of the heavens and earth*, and Pelles, Eleazer, and the three knights fell on their knees.

Lifting the Grail from its altar, Joseph approached Galahad and stood before him. A pair of seraphs raised him, and Joseph placed the chalice in his hands. "Take the Sangreal to Sarras, the Isle of Abraham, and it will return to its mine."

As Pelles and Eleazer uttered their farewells, Joseph and the seraphs led Galahad, Percival, and Bors to the seashore, where a marvelous ship awaited them. This was the vessel anciently constructed by Bilqis and Solomon in anticipation of the present moment.

Joseph directed Galahad to lie in the bed under the three spindles, white, red, and green. Percival and Bors stood at the prow. Joseph and the seraphs voiced their benedictions, and the ship set sail.

He gazed beyond life's turbid veil
In sleep as cavernous as death.
While snug like Jonah in the whale,
He saw the vision shown to Seth.

Over the centuries a city had sprung up around Abraham's citadel in Sarras, and the sacred character of the island had undergone a lugubrious eclipse. The current king of the city was a tyrant. When news reached him of the newly arrived knights, he consigned them to prison. Having done this, he fell ill, and his illness worsened as the year wore on. Just before breathing his last, he released the innocent knights and tendered his regret. The trio absolved him, and the citizenry acclaimed Galahad their new sovereign.

But Galahad had other aims:
He longed to see the Face of God.
Let others play the world's games,
He had no use for crown or rod.

Galahad secluded himself in the inner sanctum of Abraham's citadel for forty days, fasting and intoning the Name of the Deity. Day by day, his body underwent rarefaction. The Grail too, poised on the altar before him, was becoming insubstantial.

On the final night of his seclusion, when all of Sarras was cloaked in silence, a cylinder of forest-green light descended on the cell. The Grail slowly ascended the shaft, with Galahad floating after it. The chalice rose through churning vapors, diurnal and nocturnal skies, storms of stars. Presently it halted on the jutting crag of an intricately faceted, translucent peak.

Here bulked the great foundation stone,
The timeless, placeless Emerald Rock,
The pinnacle of Heaven's cone,
The door at which Truth's lovers knock.

Michael stood hard by. Galahad bowed low. With gentle but resolute hands Michael seized the Grail, kneaded it into plasticity, and pressed it into a cavity in the rock face.

In Malakut, Iblis closed his eyes and drew a profound breath. A tear in the tissue of his heart began to mend.

The mercy of the Deity
Does not exclude a single soul,
And every being at last will see
The kindness of the Source and Goal.

In Jabarut, a soul of vast destiny commenced descent. The Paraclete would soon be born.

The Year of the Elephant

Figments are a curious phenomenon. Sparks and flares from the font of existence innervate them; invigorated, they swell with verve. Sometimes the figment is content to simply gambol in the celestial froth. Its delight is delightful. Another struts in the pride of believing itself a favored child of the Deity, but goes no further. No harm done. And then there are those whose dilation emboldens them to amass addled acolytes by means of sly impostures and misrepresentations in the realm of revelation. The Diwan is then compelled to intervene.

A mind is drawn to worship God;
It's then an archon sees its prey.
By artifice and subtle fraud,
The cad now leads the soul astray.

Jesus did much to diminish the influence of devious figments, and his example brought home to a number of archons the error of their ways and the possibility of another mode of life. Those that persisted in miscreancy now saw the necessity of taking special precautions. They resolved to unite their efforts and mutually invest in a terrestrial headquarters. And where better to huddle than at the Kaaba, the ancient shrine of Adam, Eve, Abraham, and Hagar, now an idol gallery doing bustling trade, its altar lifted up to Mammon?

The figments found a choice redoubt,
The planet's oldest house of prayer.
They'd put the cherubs all to rout
And make the Cube their common chair.

In the climate of spiritual nescience prevailing in Mecca, the gentlemanly sheik 'Abd al-Muttalib cut an unusual figure. Few in the city shared his commitment to the venerable path of Abraham, and many regarded his antiquarianism with thinly concealed contempt. To their minds, the Deity was the most inchoate of abstractions; the idols that filled the Kaaba, by contrast, were solid facts eliciting splendidly solid jingling coins.

Still and all, when 'Abd al-Muttalib discovered a hidden source of water a stone's throw from the hallowed Cube, everyone was positively impressed. This, he declared, was Hagar's immemorial well. Interest in the old legends momentarily surged, though not to a degree that might endanger the city's financial interests.

The Meccans did, however, regard their prospects as genuinely jeopardized by a cathedral recently erected in Aksumite Yemen, the likes of which the world had never seen. The figments proposed an act of desecration, and a zealous Meccan obligingly made his way to Yemen to defile the church.

When faith becomes a tool of greed
And empathy concedes the match,
An archon has usurped the creed
And miseries are sure to hatch.

Abraha, Aksum's viceroy in Yemen, was furious, as he had good reason to be. But he took matters too far. Mustering an enormous army with an elephant at its head, he marched on Mecca with the intention of razing the Kaaba. In fairness, the figments had deprived the Kaaba of its holy character, but a great restoration was soon to come, and the destruction of the Cube would have been a disastrous offense. An intimation from the Deity to that effect reached the Diwan, and the ministers sprang to action.

The Deity dispatched a word:
The Diwan mobilized en bloc.
Their ally was a faithful bird
Who had, at call, a loyal flock.

Abraha first realized something was wrong when the elephant halted at Mecca's outskirts and refused to take another step. Every attempt at inducement failed, compelling Abraha to abandon the stubborn pachyderm and proceed without him.

But now the sky darkened. A thousand wings roiled the air. And suddenly it was raining stinging stones. A myriad of talons were discharging their burdens. Bloodied and battered, Abraha's men scattered, never to return to Mecca again.

That was the year Muhammad was born.

The Shining Lamp

Once, when his years could still be counted on one hand, Muhammad was tending sheep behind his nursemaid's house. It all happened so quickly. Two strangers clad in white gently took hold of him and lowered him to the ground. With nimble movements they drew out his heart, cleaved it open, and removed a clot of black blood. They had with them a tray of snow; with the icy slush they washed the extracted organ, continuing until every trace of residue was expunged. They then restored Muhammad's heart to its place, mended the incision, and took their leave without a word.

His soul was pure as pure can be,
But bodies carry ancient pains.
The seraph doctors came to free
His chest from history's dark stains.

As his father died before he was born, followed by his mother while he was still young, Muhammad was raised under the roofs of his grandfather 'Abd al-Muttalib and uncle Abu Talib.

A trader by profession, Abu Talib once took Muhammad on a commercial voyage to Syria. In Busra, the caravan paused near the hermitage of a Christian cenobite named Bahira. Observing a cool wisp of cirrus persistently hovering over Muhammad, Bahira took a special interest in the boy. When a chance arose,

Bahira asked to see Muhammad's back. There, between his shoulders, was the mark the monk had hoped to find: the seal of prophecy, sign of the Paraclete. Bahira brought out a sash that had belonged to Jesus and the elder prophets, and reverently presented it to Muhammad.

The Christ had used this sash to gird
The waist of Simon; thus it was
A legacy of Allah's Word,
A blessèd, consecrated gauze.

In his twenty-fifth year, Muhammad again traveled to Syria, this time as the agent of Khadija, a prosperous and noble lady of Mecca. Muhammad impressed her so favorably she proposed marriage, to which he agreed. As Khadija's husband and a glowing model of virtue and gnosis, Muhammad steadily rose to prominence in Meccan society. Wielding his waxing influence, he initiated a chivalrous league sworn to protect victims of injustice and bring rogues to account for their peccancies.

The Federation of Fuzul,
A league of knightly cavaliers,
Stood up to cutthroat, thief, and ghoul,
Equipped with light from higher spheres.

The rebuilding of the Kaaba gave rise to a bitter quarrel among the clans of Muhammad's tribe, the Quraysh. Each group asserted its own claim to the honor of lifting the Black Stone into position. Just when bloodshed seemed imminent, Muhammad entered through the gate. He advised the disputants to place the stone on a cloak to be lifted by the clans collectively. This done, he gently set the stone in place himself.

Each felt their rivals should be banned
And they alone should win the day.
But Ahmad called on every hand*
And all agreed this was the way.

The figments perceived a threat to their entrenchment. Some departed forthwith; others dug in their heels.

With increasing compulsion, Muhammad found himself called to the wilderness. Outside the city loomed the "Mountain of Light," so called because its substance consisted entirely of igneous rock drenched in lapping tides of solar, lunar, and stellar illumination. There, in a cave facing Mecca, Muhammad could frequently be found intoning the Name of the Deity.

Alone he sat with the Alone,
Enfolded in the depths of night,
Secluded in a cell of stone—
And light irradiated light.

While Muhammad was engaged in this manner one evening, Gabriel entered the cave and said, "Recite!"

Muhammad replied, "I am not a reciter."

In a flash Gabriel encircled Muhammad, inducing an intensity Muhammad could hardly endure. Twice again Gabriel instructed "Recite!" and enveloped Muhammad to overwhelming effect. When Gabriel released Muhammad for the third time, revelation began to flow.

Recite in the Name of your Liege, Who created
Created humans from a clot
Recite! And your Liege is the Most Generous

Who taught by the pen
Taught humans what they knew not.

Muhammad feared a jinn had bewitched him, and fled the cave. As he descended the mountain, Gabriel's form bodied forth on every horizon. The archangel's words were succinct and to the point: "Muhammad, you are the Messenger of God and I am Gabriel."

Reaching home, Muhammad asked Khadija to cover him in a cloak. When the extremity of his awe subsided, he recounted what he had witnessed. Khadija reassured him and hailed him as an honored recipient of the Deity's message. From that day, Muhammad's body functioned as a gong reverberating with vibrations welling up from the fathomless depths of reality.

The sweat-beads dripping from his curls,
As revelation shook his frame,
Were limpid opalescent pearls
In which fresh dew was wed to flame.

The revival of Abraham's religion in Mecca attracted grateful devotees, but also vituperative detractors. Muhammad's way was irenic; nonetheless, his enemies were implacable. A certain lady of the city invariably hurled offal at him when he passed under her balcony. One day she failed to appear, prompting him to make earnest inquiries in regard to her health.

Although she chose to play the pest,
He kept a place for her within
The heart that glowed inside his chest;
In fact, all souls were lodged therein.

Ascension

One night, Muhammad betook himself to the Kaaba for prayer, finally succumbing to sleep in front of the Cube. He woke with a start; above him stood Gabriel. The archangel led Muhammad to the courtyard gate. Waiting there was a silver pegasus with a radiant human face: Buraq.

A mule, yes—a donkey too,
And equally a sort of bird,
Such was the steed by which he flew
To hallowed Quds, or so I've heard.

With lightning speed, Buraq conveyed Muhammad to Jerusalem, alighting on the plaza fronting what had been the Temple of Solomon, latterly that of Herod. Physically the Temple was a desolate ruin; etherically it endured exquisitely intact. Muhammad entered among an assembly of prophets and prophetesses and proceeded to lead the congregation in prayer.

The bowing shapes were manifold,
Like pulses flashing from the sun,
Yet in the end, if truth be told,
In essence all of them were one.

A delegation from the Diwan arrived, offering Muhammad his choice of three goblets. The first contained water, the second, wine, and the third, milk. Muhammad intuitively selected the milk, to the unreserved approbation of the delegates.

He chose the milk, the symbol of
The sweetness of a mother's heart.
He chose the way of tender love,
Compassion's providential art.

At a gesture from Gabriel, Muhammad once again took to the saddle. This time the itinerary indicated by the archangel was celestial rather than terrestrial. Past tuffets of cumulus, Buraq carried Muhammad into the upper atmosphere, then beyond, into interplanetary space. Otherworldly scenes resolved and dissolved in kaleidoscopic succession: outlandish jinnic landscapes, abysses of perdition, spheres of glory, bewildering polychromatic fractal geometries.

Gabriel now led Buraq to descend at the foot of a buckthorn. The tree was apparently no different from any other member of its kind; still, somehow, it was breathtaking. In its presence, the countenances of Gabriel and Buraq, already resplendent, underwent a marvelous transfiguration, growing brighter and more ravishingly beautiful than words can convey.

A gold patina tinted all,
The dust of Heaven's finest rose,
A glory-giving royal shawl,
Becalming nature's ancient throes.

◀ *Past tuffets of cumulus, Buraq carried Muhammad into interplanetary space.*

Gabriel and Buraq could go no further, but Muhammad pressed on beyond the tree. The Deity was intensely near.

Muhammad exclaimed, "There is no god but You, the Only Being!"

A voice answered, "True, true!" And then, in a weighty whisper, "But for you I would not have created the universe."

Silence.

Self-consciousness departed from Muhammad, and the Face of the Deity shone unveiled.

The universe now disappeared
And only God Most High remained.
Muhammad's holy heart was seared,
And ardent union was attained.

Sophia's People

The harassment of the Quraysh compelled Muhammad and his devotees to remove themselves to Yathrib—Medina, as it is now called—where Muhammad was elected to lead the city. For a time an uneasy truce existed between Mecca and Medina. When the Quraysh broke the truce, Muhammad and his followers returned to Mecca as its conquerors.

The moment had now come for Muhammad to exorcize the Kaaba of its ghosts. With swift strokes he demolished the idols in which archons nefariously lurked. The only effigy he preserved was an icon of Jesus and Mary.

When you expect an honored guest
It's time to take your broom in hand.
You mustn't have a moment's rest
Until the house is spick-and-spanned.

Muhammad's terrestrial life was now nearing its end. His closest companions were his cousin 'Ali, his fathers-in-law Abu Bakr and 'Umar, and his son-in-law 'Uthman. On the night of his Ascension, Muhammad had received a celestial robe. He now asked each of his companions how they would make use of such a garment if it should come into their keeping.

Abu Bakr, 'Umar, and 'Uthman each gave suitably pious

answers. When 'Ali's turn came, he said, "Messenger of God, I would cover myself with it, I would visualize the visible with the generosity of the invisible, and I would abstain from troubling anyone."

When Gabriel heard 'Ali speak,
The angel then and there made clear
There was no need to further seek
A saint to serve as Earth's amir.

Alas, the years following Muhammad's return to the spirit world saw bloody strife between his followers. Abu Bakr succumbed to illness, but villainous assassins took the lives of 'Umar, 'Uthman, and 'Ali.

Even so, for the Arabs it was a time of headlong expansion. The Roman and Sasanian empires were tottering in decay; the animation churning out of Arabia swept into the breach, transforming the world almost overnight.

What can be said of the Umayyad and Abbasid dynasties? They persecuted the Prophet's own family. There is no gainsaying it.

Still, for all their deplorable crimes, the Umayyads and Abbasids realized certain notable achievements. The Abbasids sponsored a House of Wisdom where polymaths painstakingly concocted an innovative pantology from Indian, Greek, Persian, and Babylonian sources.

Baghdad was now, for all to see,
Old Alexandria's true heir:
The axis of philosophy,
And erudition's deepest lair.

But we are speaking here of only one variety of knowledge. The brain and the heart each have their modes of cognition and cogitation.

The philosophers are possessors of magnificent cerebrums; their gray matter thrums with methodical activity. The people of the heart think differently; their thought is the ecstasy of the moth reeling around the flame. They are called Sufis.

All of the prophets and prophetesses are their teachers. The immortal Khizr is their guide. The Diwan is their directorate. The Deity is their infinitely beloved sine qua non.

The Sufis live for God alone;
They have no other impetus.
Their bodies may be skin and bone,
And yet their hearts are limitless.

Let me name a few of them.

Dede Korkut. In his quest for a cure for death, angelic intimations led him to invent a new kind of lute, called the kopuz. Death can come at any time—except, it's said, when a person is engaged in plucking the strings of a kopuz.

So take a kopuz in your hand
And strum for all that you hold dear,
For Azrael declines to land
Where kopuz notes are in the air.

Rabi'a. People asked why she carried a torch in one hand and a pail of water in the other. Her reply: "To burn down the Garden and extinguish the Fire, so that people will worship God for God's own sake."

She said, "O Liege, if fear of hell
Is why I sanctify Your Name,
Then cast me from my hermit's cell
And hurl me in Gehenna's flames."

Dhu'n-Nun. He performed alchemical operations, deciphered the hieroglyphs carved on the ruined pillars of Panopolis, and listened to the Deity's whispers on the breeze.

Bayazid Bistami. He became a bird, flew for ten years, and perched on a branch of the Tree of Oneness.

Husayn bin Mansur al-Hallaj. He traveled to India and returned clad in a sadhu's loincloth. In ecstasy he uttered, "I am the Truth." He was tried and crucified for heresy.

Abu'l-Husayn an-Nuri. He learned the art of meditation from a motionless cat.

A feline form inertly sat
Before a mouse's little door,
And Nuri thought, that quiet cat
Knows less than I, yet somehow more.

Abu Sa'id al-Kharraz. He recommended looking for the Deity where opposites meet.

Seek out the One in interzones,
Where this and that are seen to blend:
Where beggars' mats and lordly thrones

◀ *Rabi'a carried a torch in one hand and a pail of water in the other.*

Admit their common cause and end.

Do not expect Sufis to call themselves Sufis. Or to wear a certain kind of robe or hat. Or to adhere to a dry-as-dust definition of religion. Expect the unexpected.

But a certain fragrance will cling to them. It's the aroma that wafts from the petals of the prodigy that grew in Paradise when the trees of Life and Knowledge mingled their saps.

And, now and then, you will discern an arresting hue playing in the recesses of the pupils of their eyes. It's the green of the Grail, of the Emerald Tablet, of jungles teeming with naguals—the green of the constantly returning springtide of life.

Epilogue

Mir Abu'l-Qasim, the tale is long and the night is short! I can say no more at this time. My tongue is weak, your ear is weary, and dawn is soon to break.

This will be our last conversation while you remain in that raddled body of yours. It won't be long now before you're wearing flesh and bone of light. The truth is, you're already wearing it, but your sagging skin is a shade over the lamp.

No disrespect intended. I imagine a body of clay is a fine thing in its way. I say "imagine" because, as you know, I've never donned one . . . for better or worse.

When you reach Malakut, we'll meet again, *insha'llah*. May I propose we venture a trek to the Basilica of the Diwan? Admission is by no means guaranteed—much depends on timing—but I should be able to pull a string or two. I expect a number of the ministers will be interested to meet you.

I don't say this to flatter you. The members of the Diwan regard every soul in existence with . . . how shall I say it . . . "love?" The word is somewhat mawkish, but it will have to do. The point is, these sages have given the breath of their breaths entirely to the Deity, and they see the Creator in every creature.

Back in Tus, Afsaneh will have all she needs and more, and in Malakut you'll be reunited with your son. He's gone through a phase of soul searching and I think you'll find him more genial.

For you, my friend, all that now remains is to recite the Deity's Name and await the coming of Azrael. I assure you, Azrael is an excellent escort, and your atoms will know contentment in the flux of soil, stream, and cloud.

Adieu!

Adieu.

Glossary

Unusual terms and, additionally, terms used in a manner specific to the cosmology of this work, are listed below in bold face and briefly defined. Arabic equivalents appear in italics. Words in upper case serve as cross-references to other entries.

Ahmad. The name of the prophet Muhammad prior to his earthly incarnation.

Angel. A *malak*, a denizen of JABARUT.

Archimage. A MAGUS of high degree.

Astrolatry. Star worship, a theological system in which stars are regarded not as conduits of the One's light but as archons to whom sacrifices are due.

Bakshic. Related to the methods of a bakshı, a shaman of the steppe.

Bulbul. A nightingale, known for its plaintive song.

Diaphane. An etheric, or pneumatic, body (*nasama*). A diaphane may provide the morphological template for a physical body or, as in the case of ELEMENTALS, may subsist independently of a material expression.

Diwan. The High Council of Heaven (*mala al-aʿla*), also known as the Cloud of Witnesses or Spiritual Hierarchy.

Eidolon. A body of imaginative substance (*jism-i mithali*) proper to MALAKUT.

Elemental. An *'unsuri*, a JINN embodied in a DIAPHANE.

Fae. An etheric being, whether ELEMENTAL or ORIONID.

Figment. An egregore (*sanam*), a mental formation arising from convergent SCINTILLAS in their interplay with emanations (*tajalliyat*) from the Deity; becomes an archon when animated by a malefic intelligence.

Gnome. An ELEMENTAL of earth.

Gopi. A female cowherd of India's pasturelands.

Great Epiphany. The *tajalli al-a'zam*, the central manifestation of the Godhead.

Gymnosophist. "Naked philosopher," a yogi capable of feats of concentration that open pathways to MALAKUT, JABARUT, and the silence beyond.

Hesperidia. The Americas.

Hesperidian Ocean. The Atlantic Ocean.

Hurakhsh. The angelic intelligence of the Sun.

Illiyin. A region of JABARUT.

Jabarut. The spiritual (*ruhani*) world, inhabited by ANGELS.

Jinn. A denizen of MALAKUT.

Kalim Allah. "The One Who Speaks with God," Arabic epithet of Moses.

Karshipt. The name of Jamshid's corvid mentor.

Kairos. The period in which a certain work may be auspiciously accomplished.

Khagan. Khan of Khans, emperor of the steppe.

Magus (pl. magi). A MYSTAGOGUE; originally, a Median priest.

Malakut. The World of Images (*'alam al-mithal*), inhabited by JINNS.

Marij. The smokeless fire that comprises the astral substance of MALAKUT.

Midrashim. Learned commentaries on Hebrew scripture.

Mu. Lemuria, the great lost continent of the OCEAN OF KIWA.

Mystagogue. The preceptor of a mystery school. The Greeks traced their mysteries to Egypt; Egypt inherited its mysteries from Atlantis.

Mystes (pl. mystai). An initiate in a mystery school.

Near One. *Muqarrib*, an ANGEL of the first order.

Nous. A body of spiritual substance (*jism-i ruhani*) proper to JABARUT.

Numen. The spirit of a thing or place.

Ocean of Kiwa. The Pacific Ocean.

Omphalos. "Navel," a wellspring of chthonic energy serving as the sacred center of a tradition or culture.

Oneiromancer. An interpreter of dreams auguring imminent destinies.

Orionid. A hybrid of ELEMENTAL and human, a nephil (pl. nephilim).

Perfect Nature. The actualized wholeness (*tiba' at-tamm*) of a being, integrating its various organs on all planes of existence.

Pranic. Composed of prana, etheric.

Psychopomp. A representative of the DIWAN tasked with guiding newly arrived souls through the terrain of MALAKUT.

Rum. Europe.

Sacerdotal. Priestly, or pertaining to the sacred. The sacred/profane distinction appeared with Adam and Eve's exit from the Garden and retains relevance in the absence of the Edenic state.

Sakina. Shekhina, a holy two-headed wind representing the Cosmic Person; Sophia.

Salamander. An ELEMENTAL of fire.

Scintilla. A *muwakkil*, a unit of imaginative thought.

Shahanshah. King of Kings, title of Persian and Persianate emperors.

Sibyl. A seeress, able to see into MALAKUT and JABARUT.

Species-Sovereign. A *rabb an-naw'*, a being who serves as the archetype and protector of a particular class of creatures.

Subhanallah. "Glory be to God."

Sylph. An ELEMENTAL of air.

Syzygy. A constellation of souls bound by a common destiny and subliminal mutual communion.

Tengri. The Altaic name for the Deity.

Thaumaturge. A worker of wonders or illusionist.

Theriomorphism. The technique of projecting an etheric double in the form of an animal.

Tricosm. The mesh consisting of the physical world (Nasut), the imaginative world (MALAKUT), and the spiritual world (JABARUT).

Undine. An ELEMENTAL of water.

White Sea. The Mediterranean Sea.

Yunan. Greece.

Zu'l-Qarnayn. "He of the Horns," sobriquet of Oghuz Khan.